er books by Wayne Teasdale

The Mystic Heart:
Universal Spirituality in the World's Religions

A Monk in the World:
Cultivating a Spiritual Life

Ot

[The

Discovering

[The Mystic Hours]

A Daybook of Interspiritual
Wisdom & Devotion

WAYNE TEASDALE

New World Library
Novato, California

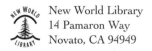 New World Library
14 Pamaron Way
Novato, CA 94949

Cover design by Mary Ann Casler
Interior design by Tona Pearce Myers

Library of Congress Cataloging-in-Publication Data
Teasdale, Wayne.
The mystic hours : a daybook of interspiritual wisdom & devotion
/ Wayne Teasdale.
    p.   cm.
ISBN 1-57731-472-7 (hardcover : alk. paper)
1. Mysticism. 2. Spiritual life. 3. Religions. I. Title.
BL625.T433 2004
204'.32 — dc22   2004013675

First printing, November 2004
ISBN 1-57731-472-7

 Printed in Canada on 100% postconsumer waste
recycled paper

g A proud member of the Green Press Initiative

Distributed to the trade by Publishers Group West

10   9   8   7   6   5   4   3   2   1

[INTRODUCTION]

∼

We all remember certain aphorisms, sayings, folk wisdom, or pithy comments we encounter during our lives. Especially meaningful words will sometimes surface in our thoughts unbidden but nonetheless welcome. These deep truths are part of our spiritual formation, whether we realize it or not. Sometimes the right sentence will open us to experiences and worldviews we never imagined before. They might appear just when we need them, giving us guidance, courage, vision, and inspiration. They are seeds of wisdom that can provide direction, change, or even a course for transformation.

With *The Mystic Hours* I seek to tap into this universal source of spiritual and human wisdom, drawing on the collective experience of humanity. Here are treasures from all the great world religions. I culled from writers, poets, philosophers, scientists, novelists, politicians, saints, mystics, and everyday people. Everyone has wisdom, and everyone can pass it on to others.

This book is meant to nourish you spiritually, aesthetically, philosophically, psychologically, poetically, mystically, and especially humanly. *The Mystic Hours* doesn't simply offer a memorable quote a day, but presents wisdom that challenges the reader to grow. I hope to avoid being too didactic with my selections, yet at the same time to address the areas in which we must each evolve.

You will find many ideas and directions repeated, although usually not from the same sources. First, I wanted to demonstrate the extraordinary parallels that exist between the philosophies of the great religious and spiritual traditions. This is the true meaning of *interspiritual*. As I explored in my book *The Mystic Heart,* interspirituality is about identifying and embracing the mystical core or common ground of the world's religions. Finding and celebrating this common ground is one of the great spiritual undertakings of our time, both to counter the terrible abuse of religious thought for the purpose of division and to help us recognize that all the religions point to one ultimate goal: our personal realization of the mystical truth underlying all reality.

Of course, we also need constant reminding of this spiritual truth, as we face the challenges and distractions that lead us to stray from the spiritual path. So in *The Mystic Hours* we will return to themes repeatedly — the themes we need to reflect on and apply in our lives, themes that need reinforcement through reintroduction. This book is actually a teaching vehicle, a raft of divine wisdom. Its focus is the whole picture of our moral, spiritual, intellectual growth. Our growth means becoming the exquisite persons we are all capable of becoming. It means discovering the radiant beings we already are as likenesses of the Divine — the Buddha-nature we already are, if we could only realize it.

Although the title *The Mystic Hours* refers to the Benedictine rule of fixed-hour prayers, in which particular prayers are prescribed for particular hours of the day, the format of *The Mystic Hours* is much less structured. These quotations and their accompanying commentary can be read and meditated on at any time. They are not broken into days or months, but rather simply numbered, one to three hundred sixty-five. This is one way to emphasize the timeless quality of these aphorisms, sayings, proverbs, or statements. I believe they are applicable to every age and every human situation.

These statements cover a vast amount of human wisdom, learned through countless millennia. They explore notions of compassion, selfless love, joy, kindness, sensitivity, forgiveness, imagination, understanding, the nature of wisdom, prayer, contemplation, meditation, suffering, learning. Each quotation is followed by a paragraph of commentary. I have drawn these wisdom seeds from everywhere, although I would particularly like to thank Michael Toms and his superb New Dimensions Radio for some of the quotations of his guests. While all the aphorisms, statements, or sayings come from others, the commentaries are my own. I hope they provide encouragement for the reader's journey.

In the Christian Contemplative tradition we have

an ancient practice called *Lectio Divina,* literally meaning "divine reading." In this form of spiritual reading,
the point is inspiration rather than information.
Through this practice, we seek to absorb just enough
information to inspire and motivate us to grow. The
lectio approach includes four levels or moments: reading, reflection, a movement in the depths of our being
called prayer of the heart, and rest or contemplation. It
is best to emphasize reading and reflection either in the
early morning before starting the day's activities, or at
night. After reading, let the absorbed ideas churn in
your heart. Of course, how you follow this method can
be modified endlessly. The point is to assist genuine
inspiration, however it is achieved.

Let each seed of wisdom take root in your being.
The objective is to derive the greatest benefit from each
statement, to allow each statement to nourish you throughout the day and beyond. These seeds of realization
together form an underlying unity. The aim is your ultimate transformation, the actualization of your higher
spiritual, aesthetic, moral, intellectual, and human qualities. May you find joy and contentment in this companion
on your spiritual journey.

— Wayne Teasdale
Chicago, Summer 2004

[The Mystic Hours]

[1]

The greatest accomplishment in life
is to be who or what you are,
and that is what God wanted you to be
when he created you.

— Abbot Thomas Keating

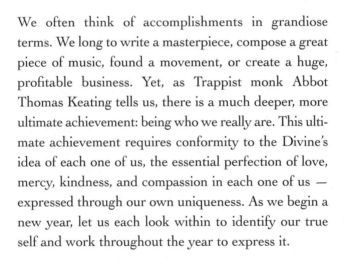

We often think of accomplishments in grandiose terms. We long to write a masterpiece, compose a great piece of music, found a movement, or create a huge, profitable business. Yet, as Trappist monk Abbot Thomas Keating tells us, there is a much deeper, more ultimate achievement: being who we really are. This ultimate achievement requires conformity to the Divine's idea of each one of us, the essential perfection of love, mercy, kindness, and compassion in each one of us — expressed through our own uniqueness. As we begin a new year, let us each look within to identify our true self and work throughout the year to express it.

[2]

I have not worshipped God from fear of his fire,
nor for love of his garden,
so that I should be like a hireling;
rather, I have worshipped him
for love of him and longing for him.

— Rabi'a al-Adawiya

Rabi'a al-Adawiya of Basra (d. 801), a Sufi and one of the early women in Islamic mysticism, identifies the motivation that characterizes the true Sufi, the genuine mystic of most traditions. One follows the Divine not out of fear, or a desire for the rewards of paradise, but because one is in love with God and is impassioned with his presence everywhere, especially within. Only the pure motive moves the Divine, and only such an intention marks the authentic mystic. May we each strive for such purity of motive and the single-minded determination revealed by the sage of Basra.

[3]

*I have found my Heaven on earth,
because Heaven is God and God is in my heart.*
— Blessed Elizabeth of the Trinity

Contrary to some more literal notions of God, the God-head dwells within the depths of our inner lives, our subjectivity. So said Blessed Elizabeth of the Trinity, a mid-twentieth-century Carmelite nun. Equally so, we dwell within the Divine subjectivity. We experience a mutual indwelling in each other. Heaven is much more than a place; it is the utter reality of God. If we are united with the Godhead in this life — the truest defini-tion of the mystical experience — then we are already in Heaven. Let us enter Heaven aright through the real-ization of God's presence in us.

[4]

Holy is the
supernatural extra brilliant kindness of the soul.

— Allen Ginsberg

This great American poet of the Beat generation, who embraced a wild Buddhist mysticism in his life and poetry, here identifies the ultimate quality that spiritual practice refines in us: utter kindness. Every saint of every faith tradition espouses it and indeed actualizes it in his or her life. If you want to know with immediate and tangible recognition what God is like, examine kindness in yourself and others. It is your own deepest inner nature. It only has to be revealed. Let us discover in ourselves this heart animated by kindness.

[5]

Stillness is the greatest revelation.

— Taoist proverb

⁓

Silence, the quiet calm at the heart of nature, carries, or even hides, the presence of the Divine. Cloaked in the stillness, the Way, the Divine One dwells, always available to us through our surrender. All we need do is dispose ourselves to listening intently. This intent listening is the essence of meditation. If we lean our ear toward the stillness, the outer quiet, it will lead us into a realization of the Presence around us, within us, and beyond us. Outer or surrounding stillness will deliver us to the inward stillness, the ultimate presence in which we really reside. Eventually, as our listening and practice mature, outer and inner finally collapse into each other, and we find ourselves in the One.

[6]

While the scientist burdens himself with facts and figures,
the sage becomes empty so that all knowledge
can pass through him
without it affecting his experience of Oneness.
While the scientist limits and narrows his vision,
the sage expands and embraces the entire universe.
The scientist sees many — the sage sees One.

— Mata Amritanandamayi

The hugging mystic Mata Amritanandamayi, or Ammachi, a Hindu guru, stresses the fundamental distinction between relative knowledge and absolute knowledge found in all traditions of mystical truth. It is the difference between mere knowledge and ultimate wisdom, between conditioned existence and the unconditioned, eternal reality. The scientist who remains concerned only with the empirical, no matter how brilliant he or she is, can only know facts confined to time and space, while the sage opens to the Ultimate Mystery and knows it from within divine unity. Truly so knowing, the sage encompasses the totality.

[7]

The choice is between nonviolence and nonexistence.
— Martin Luther King, Jr.

⌒

The eloquent simplicity of this self-evident statement almost defies commentary. King shows how what many perceive as a lofty ideal will in the end prove to be a crucial necessity, especially in light of the sobering reality of nuclear weapons and globalized terror. Reason, common sense, and the enduring wisdom of our great religions call us to the realization of our responsibility to embrace this course if we want to survive as a species in a larger community of species. Nonviolence summons us to the clear recognition that we are a fragile human family in a fragile world. In a very real sense, our choice is really between inner growth and destruction.

[8]

For the person whose mind is well trained
in the ways that lead to light,
who surrenders the bondage of attachments
and finds joy in his freedom from bondage,
who free from the darkness of passions
shines pure in a radiance of light,
even in this mortal life
he enjoys the immortal Nirvana.

— The Dhammapada

The spiritual journey in each tradition summons us beyond our slavery to our passions and desires. Part of the process of enlightenment, of awakening, is the understanding that our attachments hold us back from experiencing true happiness. Freeing ourselves from the bondage of attachment requires a mind trained in the pursuit of liberation, a mind able to let go of all that hinders one from pursuing the light of Nirvana, the path that ultimately leads to immortality.

[9]

*If the host [or hostess] would prepare the house,
there is no doubt the Guest will come.*

— St. Teresa of Avila

The gift of divine union is a treasure God wishes to give to each one of us. If we seek the Divine Presence, that is, if we prepare the house of our own being, the Guest, who is God, will come. All we have to do is work at it; we have to prepare the house by living a committed spiritual life, putting aside time each day for prayer, and most of all practicing compassion and love.

[10]

God is a substance with an infinite number of attributes....
We human beings only know two of them:
thought and extension.

— Spinoza

Spinoza, a rationalist philosopher, glimpsed something
that can only inspire deeper humility in all of us. The
Divine Reality — the Source of Being, Allah, the Brahman, the Tao, the One, the Ground of Being — has a
limitless number of qualities; each one of these is itself
infinite, but each also expresses the one nature. We have
only been exposed to two of them: thought, or consciousness, and extension — the infinite space around
us. What do we do with this knowledge? There is only
one course: surrender to the Mystery. We will never
grasp God as we would a mathematical formula, a science, a novel, or a poem. Before this truth we are sum-
moned to intellectual humility, and the conclusion that
we know precious little about God, or for that matter
existence. Let us cultivate this humility and seek refuge
in its practical wisdom.

[11]

I know that Great Person
of the brightness of the sun
beyond the darkness.
Only by knowing him
one goes beyond death.
There is no other way to go.

— Svetasvatara Upanishad

This passage from the Svetasvatara Upanishad inci-
sively focuses our attention on the personal nature of
existence — that life is not an abstract, impersonal
process, but requires engagement with the Divine in its
approachable reality. It is not sufficient to know the
Ultimate as a principle merely in an intellectual sense.
Each of us has to pass through its experience, in our
own way, and in our own tradition, if we have one.
Everything in this cosmos is incarnated here, including
God, or infinite awareness. May you have the delight
of knowing that Great Person beyond the darkness
who leads to immortality.

[12]

Mind-ocean, mind-born waves —
many unconscious ones drown.
Kabir says, he is saved
whose heart can discern.

— Kabir

The mind is essential to achieving awareness, but it can also entrap unwary souls who place too much trust in its judgment. Paradoxically, this is especially true when a person is caught in the vortex of skepticism and cleverness. Skepticism as a life choice is the way of non-commitment; it never results in recognizing the truth. It is only with the heart that we can really discern what wisdom requires of us. If we follow that intuitive source, we will save ourselves from drowning in the mind's abstractions, questions, and excuses.

The Christian is called to see all reality
with the eyes of Christ.

— John Main

⌒

To follow the admonition of the British pioneer of Christian meditation John Main is a tall order. It requires daily examination of one's intention, carefully examining one's thoughts and words and contemplating actions in the light of the Gospel. To see everything as Christ would demands that one view everything through the values of faith and hope, and particularly through love, or *agape*. Living in this way is to be part of the Kingdom of Heaven, a place that is established eternally in Divine love itself. If a person lives, thinks, and is motivated by this intention of love, of compassion, kindness, and mercy, then that person is already in God's kingdom. Christians, and those who simply admire Christ's teachings, are fortunate to have such a personal example of love to follow. Each one of us is capable of this commitment.

[14]

The first peace, which is the most important,
is that which comes within the souls of people
when they realize their relationship,
their oneness with the universe and all its powers,
and when they realize that at the center of the universe
dwells the Great Spirit and that this center
is really everywhere, it is within each of us.

— Black Elk

Sharing a remarkable philosophical parallel with Hindu thought, the great Native American medicine man from the Oglala Sioux Black Elk here describes the process of spiritual awakening, which he calls "the first peace." Attaining harmony with the Source happens naturally when we are in relationship with it, a relationship characterized by the deepest sense of oneness. In being one with the Divine, or what the Native Americans of the plains might call the Great Spirit, we are also at the center of the cosmos. In relationship with the Great Spirit, we share this same center. Let us find peace in this unity.

[15]

My religion is kindness....
I'd rather be kind than right....
You can always be kind.

— Tenzin Gyatso, the Fourteenth Dalai Lama

Kindness, which the Dalai Lama's Tibetan Buddhist tradition identifies as the refinement of compassion, is an eternal absolute. It is the bond connecting all beings in the great web of interdependence in which we all participate and by which we are sustained. A significant part of enlightenment is the awakening to this vision, at once so simple and profound — the ideal of ethics, faith, and mystical sight. Everything is encompassed by its power, necessity, and effectiveness. When we are living in harmony with our nature then we cannot resist being kind, loving, passionate, and merciful. As the Dalai Lama frequently reminds those caught up in complicated philosophies of religion, this essential fruit of the spiritual quest is the substance of his tradition.

"Hope" is the thing with feathers —
That perches in the soul —
And sings the tune without the words —
And never stops — at all —

— Emily Dickinson

Hope is a theological virtue because it concerns our destiny in relation to the Divine. This deep, timeless intuition that, ultimately, all things will turn out well is one of our primary links with spirit. This is hope that dwells in its eternal home, sending its messages from the other shore, like a gentle herald of the sacred. Hope is the voice of God in the depths of our being. Its optimism is vigorous, its vision steady, and its horizon endless. It is hope, as a guiding virtue, that grants us perspective, extending our sight beyond doubt, uncertainty, and adversity.

If we have no peace,
it is because we have forgotten
that we belong to each other.

— Mother Teresa

⌒

The world is divided enough by religions, cultures, languages, ethnicities, tribes, and nations. Even more profound are divisions between the haves and have-nots, the educated and the uneducated, those whose hearts are open and those whose hearts are closed. These crushing divisions work to isolate people and rob the world of peace. The challenge is to realize our essential interdependence, our fundamental need for one another. The key to social peace and community, indeed the key to the spiritual life, is remembrance: of God, ourselves, one another. Only when we remember our inescapable relatedness to one another will peace become a reality.

[18]

We are in touch with the highest spirit in ourselves,
we too are a Buddha, filled with the Holy Spirit,
and we become very tolerant, very open, very deep,
and very understanding.

— Thich Nhat Hanh

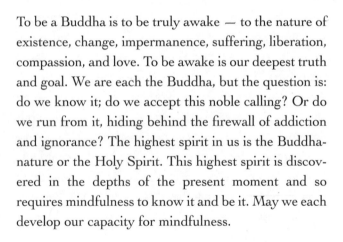

To be a Buddha is to be truly awake — to the nature of existence, change, impermanence, suffering, liberation, compassion, and love. To be awake is our deepest truth and goal. We are each the Buddha, but the question is: do we know it; do we accept this noble calling? Or do we run from it, hiding behind the firewall of addiction and ignorance? The highest spirit in us is the Buddha-nature or the Holy Spirit. This highest spirit is discovered in the depths of the present moment and so requires mindfulness to know it and be it. May we each develop our capacity for mindfulness.

[19]

Who is God? God is the meaning for my joy,
[and] a gladsome joy to my being.
— Mechthild of Magdeburg

It is God who causes joy to rise in our hearts. The compass of our mirth points to the Divine and is a revelation of its reality to us. The Source is pure bliss and we are invited to share in these inexhaustible spiritual treasures. Each one of us is made for joy, and this joy surpasses all the fleeting pleasures of this life. As they pass away, joy remains and bears us to Paradise. Cultivate joy as you would a dear friendship.

At first, before descending to this world,
the soul is imperfect;
she is lacking something.
By descending to this world,
she is perfected in every dimension.

— Moses de Leon

This Jewish mystic of the Kabbalah describes an ancient proposition found in many cultures. Many traditions regard the soul as having existed from eternity, but in a state of potentiality. It can only unfold in experience. What the soul, the abiding conscious identity, lacks is experience related to the growth of other-centeredness, or love. As many traditions such as Buddhism claim, this life, along with the experiences gained in other planes of existence, provides a kind of school in which one learns how to love in ever-expanding ranges. If we embrace this notion that life's purpose is to teach us to transcend ourselves, our tendency to put our own needs above the welfare of the community eventually dissipates.

[21]

If you would be happy all your life,
plant a garden.

— Chinese proverb

⌒

My friend Maggie is not in any way religious, but she is devoutly committed to her garden. In the warm months of the year, Maggie can be found immersed in planting, weeding, and watering. She never seems to tire of spending hours each day in her garden cloister. She derives endless contentment from this direct connection with the earth, with her immersion in the mysteries of growth, fruition, decay, and return. It is often the simple things in life that greatly enrich us and teach us things about ourselves we never knew, but they also open up for us aspects of reality that are necessary for our happiness. Let us not fritter life away in a kind of work and passive entertainment. Rather let us learn the value of contemplation in the power of the simple.

[22]

The mind is like a parachute
— it only works when it's open.

— Lily Tomlin

❧

Genuine growth is only possible if we are open and listening. A closed mind is a recipe for stagnation and mediocrity. People are always threatened by change, especially if it requires them to stretch beyond feelings of security and assumptions about happiness. An open mind and an open heart are indispensable to achieving real maturity, and, even more important, becoming an agent in the happiness of others. Let us strive to keep our minds and hearts open, the openness that education engenders and spirituality develops.

[23]

The great ancient Greek philosopher Plotinus was an extraordinary mystic. He understood that when people get immersed in this world they lose perspective. Rather than creating a false dichotomy between this world and the next, he understood that, once again, our task is to recognize, to avoid falling into a terrible ignorance. We are responsible for our ignorance, just as we all are responsible for the wisdom we acquire. Let us focus our intention on awakening to a knowledge of who we really are.

[24]

The person of (divine) knowledge is lost and buried in nothingness. While this is so, God grants him an existence from his own existence and paints him with the Divine Color.

— Ibn 'Arabi

Ibn 'Arabi (1165–1240), the Islamic philosopher and mystic, speaks to us here of the Sufi attainment of *fana,* or annihilation in God, or Allah. This teaching is very similar to that of Jesus, who exhorts his followers to lose themselves in order to find themselves. It also bears a likeness to the Buddhist notion of Nirvana, attained through the extinction of selfish desire, of self-cherishing or clinging to the self. This mystical death leads to infinite life in the Divine, beyond the nothingness of *fana,* expanding into the life of God who gives us "existence from his own existence."

[25]

All things are too small to hold me,

I am so vast.

— Hadewijch

⌒

Hadewijch (1150–1200), a Prussian nun, was the recipient of eleven mystical visions, and in the above
exclamation she reports God's own words on the divine
infinity and the human limitations in relation to him.
We simply do not have the capacity to contain, com-
prehend, or explain God. The Divine's vastness means
that God is infinitely infinite. While we humans have
infinite capacity, our experience is finite. We are not
equipped to grasp the infinitely actual being of the
Absolute. In contrast to the Ultimate's vastness, we
are so small, and yet we have ability to consider and
reflect on God's vastness or infinity. May this reflection
deepen our humility and open us more in trust to the
Divine Source.

[26]

He whose every undertaking
is free from desire and selfish purpose,
and he who has burnt all his actions
in the fire of knowledge — such a one
the wise call a sage and learned one.

— Bhagavad Gita

⁓

An enlightened person, or one well on the way, is one who has broken free from ego-based attitudes, decisions, and actions. Freed from the false self, such a person is then capable of real compassion and loving action. The Bhagavad Gita, the great Hindu holy poem that tells the story of two warring royal Indian clans, guides us toward being truly available to selfless service. Our deepest intention, it tells us, must be liberated from self-seeking action. We become sages when we understand the necessity of selfless intention and action. Only by surrendering to the way of humility, of letting go of actions for our own sake, can we leap into enlightened being. Let us strive to cultivate that quality of selflessness in our deepest intention, in our relationships and in our actions.

A true statesman is someone who is
willing to take risks for peace.

— Shimon Perez,
to Charlie Rose

As Nobel Peace Prize Laureate Shimon Perez, an elder statesman of Israel, claims here, true leadership requires the vision to guide the people along an unknown path, with the tangible hope of breaking through to a better life. The cycle of violence can only be broken when both sides realize there is no alternative to peace. A leader cannot simply be governed by the principle of playing it safe. That is not leadership, but capitulation to political expedience. The prophetic approach is always open to a new turn in the road, to taking a new risk for a change that holds promise or at least carries us one step closer to reconciliation. Let us become sober risk takers for the sake of others.

[28]

Divinity is wrapped in a robe of Light.

— Psalm 104

~

While we often hear superficial associations between mystical experience and light, we may miss the more literal truth known for millennia by countless mystics and sages. As author Peter Russell beautifully describes in his book *From Science to God*, the Divine is, in some genuine and ultimate sense, light. It doesn't simply dwell in light; it *is* light itself. When we examine the evidence more closely, we find light directly involved in everything going on in our universe and presumably all other universes. Light is consciousness in the act of revealing, of dispelling the darkness, while consciousness is light in the act of knowing and understanding. The two are interchangeable.

[29]

*Nobility is rooted in humility,
loftiness is based on lowliness.*

— Chuang Tzu

Taoist philosopher Chuang Tzu (369–286 B.C.E.) draws attention to one of the basic teachings of Taoism: humility of heart. In its beautifully paradoxical and, often for Westerners, elliptical language, Taoism is an ethics of humility based on nature mysticism, a way of life derived from close observation of the cosmos. And humility, as a principle, is operative throughout. True greatness is found in the humble disposition. It is an acceptance of reality balanced with an openness to positive change. Nature teaches us that stability of being is rooted in a very basic honesty about reality. As Chuang Tzu teaches us, the heights of experience must be grounded in the firmness of the earth. Let us strive for this noble virtue that is the basis of all the others — the foundation of good governance, the possibility of peace, and the spiritual evolution of each person.

[30]

The spiritual teacher provides a map for the path of awakening, but the student must make the journey. The ticket for enlightenment is not transferable.

— Ellen Grace O'Brian

Contemporary Hindu sage Ellen Grace O'Brian tells us that each person must walk the path himself/herself. There is something in the human psyche, and particularly in many seekers' psyches, that craves a guru to provide all the answers. Many want to follow unquestioningly, which leads to innumerable abuses. Although a teacher can point the way, this teacher, even if a true spiritual master, cannot do the work for you. Each one of us must do our own work, the labor of transformation, which takes a lifetime. Gurus can teach skills and methods — maybe even transmit mystical illumination — but the student must assimilate, process, and integrate this input. Spirituality in this sense is an exercise in inner self-reliance, since each of us is alone in the task of evolving toward enlightenment, growing in love, compassion, and kindness. The spiritual guide's role is critically important, but the student must be ready to receive the benefit of the teacher's gifts with earnestness and discipline.

[31]

There is an inmost center in us all
where truth abides in fullness.

— Robert Browning

⁓

The Victorian poet Robert Browning (1812–89) aptly
identifies that deepest, most ultimate identity within us
where we encounter truth. The mystics have many
names for it: the soul, the Atman, the spirit, the *apex
mentis,* the soul-spark, *die Funkelein,* the inner ground,
even consciousness. It is in this center, in this fine
point, that the human spirit meets the Divine Spirit.
That is a place of utter light, truth, realization, and
ecstasy. That center is the eternal now that does not
change, that transcends corruption and the vagaries
of time, the fashions of the age, and the movements of
thought. It is the task of each one of us to be established in our inmost center where we meet God, a place
where the world cannot intrude and where everything
is possible.

[32]

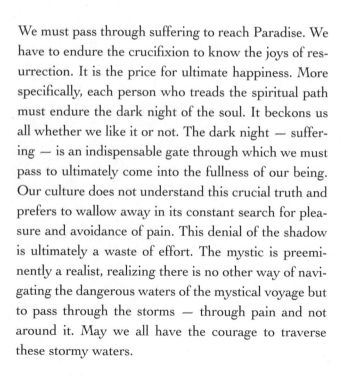

One may not reach the dawn...
save by the path of night.

— Anonymous

We must pass through suffering to reach Paradise. We have to endure the crucifixion to know the joys of resurrection. It is the price for ultimate happiness. More specifically, each person who treads the spiritual path must endure the dark night of the soul. It beckons us all whether we like it or not. The dark night — suffering — is an indispensable gate through which we must pass to ultimately come into the fullness of our being. Our culture does not understand this crucial truth and prefers to wallow away in its constant search for pleasure and avoidance of pain. This denial of the shadow is ultimately a waste of effort. The mystic is preeminently a realist, realizing there is no other way of navigating the dangerous waters of the mystical voyage but to pass through the storms — through pain and not around it. May we all have the courage to traverse these stormy waters.

*Every face you encounter in life is a face
of the Faceless One. God has a vast face.*

— Nicholas of Cusa

Nicholas of Cusa (1401–64), also known as Cusanus, was a German mystic, systematic philosopher, and cardinal. Here he offers his own version of a profound existential truth found in every tradition: The Divine One is present in every being. Mother Teresa often spoke about how she could see Christ in everyone she met. Nicholas of Cusa reminds us that being really awake means recognizing this Divine Presence in every person, and indeed in every creature or sentient being — perhaps even in every rock, blade of grass, or star. Each of us is part of the infinite reality of the Divine's face, a manifestation of its endless creativity, and each is dear to this ineffable source. When we become devoutly attentive, acting from the deep realization that everyone we meet is actually God, we never miss the Divine Presence peering out at us in the eyes of the other, and finally we become very careful in our actions, making them an expression of love and care.

[34]

Creativity happens at the boundary between order and chaos, when we're poised between the two. In our own lives, the edge is where we are constantly reinventing our culture, constantly questioning our assumptions.

— Danah Zohar

This quote from the author of *The Quantum Society* reminds us that creativity risks time, money, and even sanity. Genius often sits very close to madness, and it is this proximity that creates a space of discovery, insight, invention, and breakthrough. Creativity leads beyond the routine safety of the known. The creative spirit is never satisfied with what we know — or *think* we know — with past achievements, or the comforts that lull us into a mechanical living of life. Creativity involves stretching beyond our current understanding, attitudes, capacities, and opinions. Through creativity, culture continues to evolve on the back of innovation. It is through creativity that our social views develop and our society progresses. The creative mind is never content with our current assumptions unless they are founded on deep truth. It is in tension, polarity, contrast, and finally paradox that the new emerges.

[35]

Just as a wave on the ocean is what the ocean is doing,
you are what God is doing.

— Wayne Dyer

Each one of us is internally related to God, and we couldn't be if we were not so connected. Such a view might be regarded as pantheistic, the belief that equates God with the physical laws of the universe, but that is not the case. It really means that each one of us, indeed all sentient beings, manifests the Divine Reality. It means that our existence is not really a private matter. To *be* means essentially to be related to the Divine. We are here for a purpose that involves all of us. The Divine Reality is doing, or being, each one of us. We are expressions of God's endless creativity. The Divine is happening all the time, and in all corners of reality. The question for every one of us is this: Are we allowing God to be God in and through us?

I don't think that any great issues ever get resolved.
Rather, I think we outgrow them.

— Jean Houston

The great matters that divide us, most ironically the world's terrible conflicts over religion, are usually irreconcilable as long as the combatants are so heavily invested in their positions. One example of this kind of polarization is the terrible conflict in Northern Ireland between Catholics and Protestants. Neither side of this conflict will likely ever understand the other side's position as long as they cling to the very real injustices they have suffered. Eventually, the two sides will tire of death and hatred and will abandon the old rivalry. That we may outgrow our need for dualism and conflict — that is my prayer.

[37]

To be free of fear, one must understand death.

— J. Krishnamurti

⌒

All fear is ultimately related to death; it's our emotional reaction to the great unknown. The unknown is like a wall around perception, insight, and knowledge. We are uncertain of what is beyond this seeming barrier to existence, though many have been granted, through near-death experiences, a prophetic vision of the absolute future. Near-death studies have whittled away at the dismissive skepticism that has ignored the implications of this extraordinary phenomenon. If we attain both an intimate realization of death's absolute inevitability and an understanding that death is a doorway, a transition to a greater reality for us, our fear will dissolve. With freedom from this looming apprehension, we are made ready for life in its fullness; we exist much more comprehensively when the totality of our being is engaged. Becoming free of fear isn't easy; it requires work and facing death's reality head-on.

[38]

A weapon is an enemy even to its owner.

— Turkish proverb

⌒

The mentality that requires a weapon is dualistic, and it is an obstacle to an enlightened way of being in the world with others. It is to fall into the trap of "us against them" thinking, which sees potential enemies everywhere. It creates an environment of suspicion and distrust. This Turkish aphorism is parallel to Jesus' teaching that living violently toward others puts a person in the path to receive violence. Of course, both these statements are about karma, the moral responsibility we have for our attitudes, words, and actions. Let us daily examine our conscience when it comes to violence.

[39]

*A path that follows the heat of erotic inspiration
brings us face to face with our own dangerous wildness.*

— Harriet Eisman

⌒

Sexuality has an enormous, almost uncontrollable
power, as Harriet Eisman tells us in "That Other Love-
liness." Left to itself, it can be destructive. Its wild,
uncontrollable nature can plunge us into difficulties. To
actualize the holiness of erotic inspiration, sex must be
consecrated by commitment. Sex is holy and therefore
has to be seen as part of a spiritual order that requires
a sacred function. Without care, it can lose its ultimate
purpose as a vehicle of ever-deepening intimacy, of a
love that grows richer with time and maturity. May we
be wise about our sexuality and let it be guided by love.

[40]

Since Auschwitz we know what man is capable of.
And since Hiroshima we know what is at stake.

— Viktor Frankl

⌒

While the horrors of Nazi Germany's policy of destruction toward the Jewish people is well known, for most
people, its motives and scale remain almost completely
incomprehensible. How an educated and cultured nation
could descend into such brutalization is nearly beyond
our ability to grasp. Such sheer absence of conscience,
such cold intelligence of execution, make us shudder and
recoil in disbelief that humans could conceive of, and ca-
pitulate to, such evil. Sobering though it is, this aspect of
human nature exists and has led to genocides since
World War II, in Cambodia and Rwanda, for example.
As Holocaust survivor Viktor Frankl here hints, the
stakes have risen. Nuclear weapons and globalized terror now threaten the very survival of all life on earth.
Without moral and spiritual transformation, there is little
hope for us. Education aids the process of inner change,
but it's ultimately insufficient. Well-educated people
across the planet have carried out despicable acts. What
is required is a change in our hearts.

[41]

It is not death that is the tragedy of life...
[but] what you let die when you are alive.

— Robert Muller,
former Assistant Secretary General of the United Nations

⌒

When they are young, most people have a genuine desire to serve the world, to selflessly contribute to humanity's future and to the future of all sentient beings. Yet many become disillusioned with age and give up on their earlier desire. They settle for something less, like simply achieving the American dream. That dream isn't bad; it's just not enough to realize our potential as spiritual beings. Such persons let their purer desire die, and all the good they might have accomplished dies with it. Robert Muller never surrendered his heartfelt passion to serve, to make a difference, and he has succeeded in birthing an optimistic vision of the future. Let us all nurture, cherish, and guard the integrity of our intention to give ourselves to the demands of the future, rather than to the limited goals of materialism. Let us encourage our deepest, purest desires.

[42]

Human speech is limited. It may be profound,
rich, and imaginative, but finally it is limited.

— Diana Eck

Harvard professor of comparative religion Diana Eck here describes a professional hazard for those writing about spirituality. Language, no matter which, is simply unable to communicate an adequate and comprehensive understanding of the Divine, or of mystical experience in its full immediacy, vividness, urgency, and ultimacy. It's always circumscribed by a people's history, culture, expectations, and the bare horizon of meaning — the extent of words' meanings. In divine matters, language always falls short of the complete truth. Indeed, gestures, rituals, music, and art can often express much more than words. When exploring words, concepts, or ideas in their finitude, let us remember that we can only point to the Divine and must leave the rest to the mystery.

[43]

The one thing God doesn't have is lack.
So, what we can offer him is our need.

— Shams of Tabriz,
Sufi master

God has, and in a sense is, everything. It is only vicariously through us, when we experience want or lack, that the Divine Spirit knows need. God feels and is sensitive to our needs. Divinity is especially near the sincere tears of souls that are in distress or repentance and those that are reaching out in faith, love, and hope. The greatest need each one of us has is for the Divine itself, and if that compelling desire is pursued with single-mindedness, God cannot fail to respond to us. Jesus tells us to "knock, seek, and ask." The door will open, what is sought will be found, and what we ask for, God will give us. Jesus' teaching refers to the pure desire for relation to the Divine. If we are truly stretching ourselves in our pursuit of God, then he will reveal himself to us in everything. He always responds to this ultimate need. May we each cultivate this salutary longing.

[44]

One film can change a life forever.

— Franco Zefferelli

⌒

The Italian film director Franco Zefferelli always cultivates true beauty in his films, and for me that beauty
has been especially present in his films with religious
themes. The director made an immensely popular and
influential 1976 film entitled *Brother Sun, Sister Moon*
about the lives of St. Francis and St. Clare of Assisi. It is
a cinematic poem, with richly colorful and breathtaking
scenes of central Italy's Umbria, where the saints lived.
In a documentary about the film, Zefferelli commented
on how a film can alter one's life forever. He spoke of the
spiritual influence, the contribution to our mystical lives.
We must remember the profound influence of films —
on ourselves, our families, friends, communities, and students — when we let their images into our mind, heart,
and unconscious.

[45]

That you need God more than anything,
you know at all times in your heart.
But don't you know also that God needs you —
in the fullness of his eternity — you?...
You need God in order to be, and God needs you —
for that which is the meaning of your life.

— Martin Buber

Many who have chosen the spiritual path understand our need for the Divine, but few, writes Martin Buber in *I and Thou*, realize that God needs us. Each one of us here in this world, and all beings in every other world, in every other universe or more subtle realm, is required for God to be all in all. We all lean on God for our existence and for the continuity of being after this life, but we are all aspects of God's fuller reality and all that creation contains everywhere and at every time. It is essential that each one of us achieves our potential for holiness, wisdom, and love in our present existence, for in this way, we contribute to the Absolute's perfection in relation to created or emanated being, reality, and manifestation.

[46]

Do you need proof of God's existence?
Does one light a candle to see the sun?

— Taoist aphorism

The Divine Reality is evident to anyone who knows how to look. It is everywhere, in everything, and radiates from all beings. We can glimpse it when we really look, in the order, design, beauty, and harmony of nature. In fact, in many ways the Divine is as obvious as the sun. Sometimes what is right in front of us is difficult to grasp because it is everywhere, because we are subsumed in its context. Wherever we look there are signs, clues, images of the Divine Presence and its vast activity across space and time. It also appears in the depths of the self and the unconscious, in dreams, creativity, love, wonder, philosophical reflection, poetic inspiration, in chance meetings, and in all the little joys of life. There is no place we can look or be that we will not find God, if only we recognize what we are seeing.

[47]

All things hang like a drop of dew
upon a blade of grass.

— W. B. Yeats

⌒

With the abrupt insight of a Japanese haiku poet, the Irish poet Yeats (1865–1939) here beautifully conveys the reality of impermanence. Our lives are precious, fragile realities. Everything can fall apart and disappear overnight, like that drop of dew. In time everything will change, following the endless cycle of death and rebirth. This realization, for Americans, was more dramatically grasped after the tragedy of September 11, 2001, when the immediacy of death, so close for most of the world, horrifically broke through our usual privileges to remind us of our fragility. This wise acknowledgment is present in all the world's spiritualities, but it is often ignored in ordinary life. While Yeats reminds us of this sober truth through his beautiful natural imagery, he also offers us hope — an understanding based on a radical experience of the interdependence of all beings and realities, and also an intimate dependence on the Source.

[48]

If you're here now, you'll be there then.

— Native American aphorism

The continuity of being is inescapable. Life for all of us goes on in some form, in some place, realm, either concrete or subtle, on this planet or in another world in this universe. The mystery of death circumscribes each of our lives. Many feel, from time to time, an eternal sense of existence, the ineffable feeling of having always been. We cannot really die in any permanent way, but are ever called on from one transition to another until we are transformed. Once we know how to be here in the integrity of the moment, we enter the Eternal Now and we know we will always be. Meditation is one of the most effective ways to learn to be in the present moment and so to enter its eternal truth. Let us develop the motivation and determination to be in this most ordinary and extraordinary manner.

[49]

Gaze into the heart of each creature and kin
and behold the Beloved who gazes upon you with love.

— Sister Georgene Wilson

Franciscan nun Georgene Wilson is what is called an anchoress, a hermit living a contemplative life, in a small hermitage in Wheaton, Illinois. She is also a poet, artist, mystic, and spiritual director of souls. For Georgene, in every person and every sentient being, the Divine is expressing itself, is loving each one of us. God is the self in every person, and with the requisite sensitivity, we can discern this presence shining forth in all things. This capacity to discern the Divine Presence in all sentient beings is a hallmark of the mystic saint of every tradition. It is essential that we realize in our dealings with our fellow creatures on this planet that we all belong to the same ultimate family, one that is essentially arising from, being maintained by, and returning to the Divine Reality. In more personal terms, as we can gather from Georgene's aphorism, we can encounter the Beloved, the Holy One, in every living being.

[50]

A dream that I dream alone is only a dream,
but a dream that we dream together is reality.

— Raul Seixas

Brazilian composer Raul Seixas understands that great societal changes, whether they are far-reaching governmental reforms or the slow dismantling of a society's institutionalized racism, require vision and a movement. The civil rights struggle and the anti–Vietnam War movement are examples in American history. One individual's visionary dream can inspire another individual, a neighborhood, a nation, even the entire world. One person can lead the masses to embrace a completely new course — even one that directly opposes the status quo. When we have a worthy dream, an inspired vision, we cannot keep it to ourselves; we must share it with others if it is to catch the popular imagination and eventually become imbedded in others' collective hopes, becoming the dream of the people. Let us all dare to dream something large and put our lives behind it.

[51]

Music is the only sensual pleasure without vice.

— Samuel Johnson

⌒

Whatever we think of other sensual pleasures — whether or not we consider them vices — we can all agree that our life here on Earth would be terribly diminished without music. Music inspires, opening minds and moving hearts. Great music appeals to our emotions, stirs up feelings, aspirations, and possibilities. From grand orchestral movements to the sounds of the wind in trees and water rippling over rocks, music can touch us. It can be mundane, even pedestrian, drawing us to become totally immersed in ordinary experience. And the sacred musical forms of the world's religions are conduits of inspiration that can lift the soul to the greatest heights. Let us be aware of music's potential to lead us and inspire us. Let us allow music to carry our deepest intention.

[52]

When there is no desire, all things are at peace.

— Tao Te Ching #37

Lao Tzu, the author of the Tao Te Ching, here identifies a fundamental truth of all religious traditions: The root of all human problems is selfish desire. This extends from the inner, psychological truth of the Buddha's Four Noble Truths, where the Buddha identified how individual suffering stems from desire. Our basic need to overcome our focus on desire or craving is a pivotal insight of Buddhism. Serious students of spiritual growth and transformation will discipline personal desire and in advanced instances abandon it altogether. We can see the same principle working between people, as the Christian tradition shows, recognizing the pitfalls in selfishly seeking our own good while ignoring that of the larger community. It is also clear that genuine peace for each one of us is impossible without freedom from the governance of selfish desire. When each person is beyond such self-cherishing, the worst of what we see in corporate greed, sexual abuse, and violence falls away, and peace emerges into reality as the pervading and enduring condition. Equanimity is the gift of spiritual maturity, and spiritual maturity only happens when we are no longer controlled by our desire.

[53]

I am because we are, and because we are, I am.

— African proverb

~

This proverb expresses a simple but profound truth at the very foundation of African culture that should be re-recognized by other world cultures: We exist in community, in relationship to one another. Our individual being depends on others; we are defined by relationship. You and I and everyone have being because of others. Former Archbishop Desmond Tutu tells us that this concept in South African culture is called *ubuntu,* meaning, "A person becomes human through other persons." He calls this the opposite of our Western notion of "I think, therefore I am." In essence, it is through others that we come to an awareness of ourselves. Identity cannot be achieved in isolation from the community, but in the give and take of communication, in sharing life, and through shared culture. We desperately require a human context in order to grow, and it is only with others that we are challenged to look at our attitudes, values, and actions. Let us carefully consider the balance necessary in our lives between the individual and the community and cherish our fundamental dependence on others.

[54]

We call them saints when what we really often mean to say is "icon," "hero," ones so possessed by an internal vision of divine goodness that they give us a glimpse of the face of God in the center of the human. They give us a taste of the possibility of greatness in ourselves.

— Joan Chittister

Joan Chittister, a Benedictine nun and activist, is a prophetic figure and an example of what she reveals in her sharing. She points to the universal appeal of holy souls. Too often, people seeking spiritual truth look to their teachers for ultimate wisdom and authority, abdicating responsibility for their own decisions and progress. In fact, as Chittister claims, the saints are there for our inspiration, to point the way toward our own advancement. The saints are ordinary people who have surrendered to love, compassion, and kindness. The goodness they reflect is the Divine Goodness itself. The perfection they share is rooted in their capacity to love. Sanctity is not only a matter of knowledge or wisdom, but a shift to other-centeredness and a transformation of character, will, motivation, and understanding. Let us be inspired to walk this path to greater life, happiness, and joy — transforming the saints' holy example into our own enlightenment.

If you are to fight, fight against your own desires.

— Jain proverb

The venerable tradition of Jainism has distinguished itself in its history through its eloquent example of and teaching on *ahimsa,* nonviolence or nonharming. It has never had a war in its long history of twenty-five centuries. For Jains, nonharming is an absolute. They regard nonviolence as the supreme religion. Nothing justifies violence against any sentient being. In this aphorism, Jainism draws attention to where the real human struggle is to be found. In this, there is a parallel with the Sufi teaching that the real *jihad* is within, a struggle with ourselves against our own attitudes, blocks, and resistance to love, compassion, and kindness.

The highest wisdom is kindness.

— Berakot, 17A (Jewish tradition)

⁓

Wisdom is always a practical matter. It goes to the core of what it means to be a fully developed human being. While enlightenment, holiness, or perfection — as far as they are possible in this life — involve knowledge of a high order, they are never complete unless one's heart is engaged. That core, our center of willing and acting, undergoes a shift in which the individual is no longer exclusively focused on his/her limited goals derived from the false self, the egoistic fixation, but is committed to the welfare of others. This straightforward but powerful Jewish proverb — a beautiful echoing of the Dalai Lama's fundamental distillation of his own Buddhist path — sums up the essence of spiritual and human maturity. Genuine kindness is ever-expanding in its scope and consistency. Kindness will eventually transform the entire existence of an individual, having reverberations in the community and the world. Let us allow ourselves to be refashioned by the effective and beautiful quality of kindness.

[57]

Let us work for people and the world and serve
as representatives of the kami *[deities]*
to make society firm and sound.

— The general principles of Shinto life

When we become truly established in other-centeredness, where we put the well-being of the community above our own self-interest, then we somehow also speak and act for the Divine. We are being and acting as ambassadors for the *kami,* as the Japanese Shinto tradition puts it. To so speak, act, and be actually defines the prophet in any tradition, the one who speaks and acts for God, the one who has been appointed by God to carry on this mission in the world. The prophet — the sage, saint, or mystic — never speaks or acts from self-interest, but from surrender to the Divine Will. Of course, in the traditional Shinto society of Japan, which along with Zen Buddhism infuses that country's ancient culture, whoever is so grounded in right motivation and behavior thinks, speaks, and acts in the light of the ancestors.

[58]

In the garden of the soul,
plant the seed of the Word (the Lord's
Name). Water the soil with love and humility
and reap the fruits of divinity.

— from Guru Granth Sahib, the Sikh Scriptures

Drawing on the extended metaphor of a garden, this passage of the Guru Granth Sahib speaks of the soul's garden cultivating the living flower of the Word. Over time, the cultivation of the Divine Word in the soul's garden leads to the gifts of the Divine One. Remembering God in a constant way through prayer, chanting, or meditation, as well as compassionate, loving action, is the path to cultivating the Word. That seedling of the Word eventually grows to maturity, blossoming into an extraordinary being. The loving, humble attention to God in each moment brings a rich harvest of Divine Union, of intimacy with God.

[59]

If we want to find a true solution to the confusion,
the chaos, and the misery of the world,
we have to find it in the world itself.

— Sri Aurobindo,
Hindu philosopher

Sri Aurobindo (1872–1950) was educated in the West but became one of India's greatest philosophers and mystic sages. He had a very deep experience of the Transcendent Reality, and yet he was also focused on the immanent workings of the natural world through the evolutionary process. This statement sounds like a denial of the Christian notion of the place of grace, or the Divine Presence, but it is not. Aurobindo knew that the key to solving the world's problems was hidden in the world's own complexities, realities, and principles. All we need to know is present in the world; it is written in the nature of the earth. Let us dedicate ourselves to discovering that natural wisdom present in the world so that we can spread this awareness and change the course of the world.

[60]

There is no danger that dauntless courage cannot conquer.

— H. P. Blavatsky

Madame Blavatsky was a Russian esoteric writer and a leader of the Theosophical movement that began in the late nineteenth century. The basis of all fear is essentially the terror of death, a natural aversion we all experience. To fear is human, but it becomes a problem when it controls our lives. Courage is also a human quality and a virtue that checks, or disciplines, fear by setting it aside and not permitting it to paralyze us with inaction or indifference. Courage does not ignore danger, nor does it negate fear; it concentrates on what must be done and on the hope of something better. It is inspired by an attribute of the eternal that is willing to risk everything for the sake of overcoming obstacles that threaten the world, society, nature, the innocent, or the future. Courage is a virtue of the wise and the brave but more ultimately of the holy, the transformed, the enlightened. Mystics see the larger, indeed largest, picture, and so they have courage in the face of challenges. They feel fear, recognize danger, but act anyway.

Go placidly amid the noise and haste,
and remember what peace there may be in silence.

— The Desiderata

The anonymous wisdom of the Desiderata was found on a tombstone in the seventeenth century. While its author is unknown, it contains some of the wisest advice for those wishing to live a life of fullness in meaning, direction, and ultimate belonging. The line above represents only a fraction of the teaching of this unusual document, yet it sums up a basic strategy for a happy life: Don't get caught up in all the confusion, excitement, noise, and business of human society. It is ephemeral and often meaningless. Many things attract our precious attention, but few are worthy of our time and few fulfill the substantial needs of ourselves and others. The author also reminds us of the depth and perdurability of the peace arising from a commitment to silence. The occasions that call for silence are more common than not. Let us develop a spirit of quiet in all our interactions.

[62]

*What we often take for reality in this world
is really the play of Shadows.*

— Plato

⁓

The Greek philosopher Plato, in his monumental work *The Republic,* tells us that our notion of reality is really like the play of shadows on the wall of a subterranean cave. He speaks within the context of our limited knowledge, what we perceive in everyday life — whether it is real, illusory, or somewhere in between. Another way we can interpret his insight is that so often what we consider to be real is actually insubstantial. We often become tenaciously attached to completely inessential cultural forms. We take them so seriously, when in reality they are just entertainment and in fact a way for us to obscure other, more painful realities. But our destiny is not tied up with them, with whether a particular sports team wins or loses, for example. At some point, we may wake up and gain perspective, realizing our treasures are not nearly as important as we thought. It may not be easy to reach, much less maintain, this lofty perspective in the midst of an emotionally charged football game, but these are precisely the places where such understanding is required. Let us strive to distinguish between what is real and what are shadows on the screen of experience.

[63]

It is always the secure who are humble.

— G. K. Chesterton

⌒

G. K. Chesterton's statement could just as easily be put another way: It is the humble who are secure. The humble are secure precisely because they are humble, and the secure are secure because they have this humility of heart. The quality of security here is certainly not economic. That kind of security often leads to arrogance; it is a refuge for the false self. In fact, growing in humbleness of attitude, disposition, and action becomes more difficult as we gain more money. The security of which this British writer speaks is spiritual. It is the great strength that comes from wisdom, a practical insight into the nature of reality and what is expected of us in this life. Wisdom inspires humility, a clarity about the truth of ourselves and the reality of life, our relationships, our work, talents, defects and limitations, and our potential. The humble truly know themselves. This security is like a rock, a solid foundation that allows each one of us to become the extraordinary person we can be.

[64]

*I do not think the measure of a civilization is how
tall its buildings of concrete are, but rather how
well its people have learned to relate to their
environment and fellow human beings.*

— Sun Bear of the Chippewa tribe

Sun Bear reminds us here of the primacy of moral consciousness over scientific and technological prowess.
Civilization has produced so many wonders — the
modern state, democracy, movies, airplanes, a vast literature, amazing feats of research, modern medicine, and
the miracles of communication — but of what ultimate
value are all of these achievements if the human family
fails to conquer the false self, which could imperil its
ultimate survival? If our technological progress comes
at the price of the simple but vital task of learning to live
in harmony with the natural world and means ignoring
the importance of our primary connection with one
another, then the price is clearly too high. The care of
the earth and of one another is far more important than
anything we can create from our human ingenuity.
Nature's wholeness and our intrinsic interconnectedness are primary. Let us pay attention to these vital
areas of awareness and commit ourselves to them.

[65]

It is the easiest thing in the world
for a person to deceive himself.

— Benjamin Franklin

Ben Franklin certainly knew human nature! Self-deception is a human talent we have all practiced at one time or another — denial about our faults, our slow pace in personal growth, the danger of large and small addictions, how well we treat others. Smokers can lie to themselves that their habit won't eventually kill them. They can turn a blind eye to a thousand empirically certain studies, and they won't even listen to their own bodies. Self-deception can even extend to nations and governments, as shown by how the United States is currently deceiving itself about global warming. We deceive ourselves when we ruthlessly seek our wants or use other people to obtain them. We lie to ourselves to shield our conscience from the truth. When we deceive ourselves, we are hurting ourselves the most. Such deception leads to the creation of a false self that protects us from confronting the truth. The cure is pure honesty and humility. True humility never tolerates self-deception.

[66]

*A good end cannot sanctify evil means, nor must
we ever do evil, that good may come of it.*
— William Penn, Quaker

Ends never justify the means, as we can see from the terrible evil propagated by global terrorism. Terrorists convince themselves, through a gross misinterpretation and distortion of religious teachings, that employing murderous means to achieve political goals is not only permissible but ordained. Such thinking is the by-product of deep moral corruption. In truth, Allah is all-merciful and compassionate, as a true reading of the Qur'an will reveal. As a Sufi master from Israel remarked to me after September 11, "the terrorists think they are doing God's work, but actually they are doing the Devil's work." Let us labor for the moral clarity to grasp this Quaker wisdom and guard our consciences from any corrupt reasoning that tries to justify evil.

[67]

If you wish to possess finally all that is yours,
give yourself entirely to God and become what He is.

— Hadewijch

⁓

Hadewijch, a Christian mystic of the Middle Ages, was a woman of enormous understanding of divine matters. Here she poetically draws us to the utter necessity of detachment, of letting go of our desires so that we may seek infinite consciousness in every moment of our awareness. John of the Cross made the same point in nearly the same words. Detachment is not simply letting go of desire; it is also, paradoxically, attaching to yourself, through commitment to the Source, the conscious intention of your heart, your will, and your constant attention. If you live in this way, with a true purity of heart, all things will come to you. There is more, however, to Hadewijch's teaching: Seeking the Divine alone allows us to become who we really are and positions us to receive what is good for us, rather than what might harm us or block our greater spiritual growth. Let us make every effort to achieve this simplicity of intention in our spiritual lives.

[68]

*Time is a factory where everyone slaves away
earning enough love to break their own chains.*

— Hafiz

Hafiz, the Sufi mystical poet, here unveils an essential clue as to why we are here. He identifies this life as "time," because living in this realm of being is expressed partially as duration, and we traverse the successive unfolding of states of existence through a temporal sequence. Hafiz claims that the purpose of life's slavery in this factory of the world is to grow in our capacity to love in its fullest sense, that is, other-centeredly. Knowing that he speaks in the context of the Divine, we can be certain that God, or Allah, would only be content with a love worthy of him — a selfless love that reaches out to others in compassionate service. Only this purity of love can build up enough power to overcome the chains of illusion that hold us here. Only such love can free us from what holds us back from realizing our true potential. In this way, love will break the chains of the obstacles inside of us.

[69]

The love that binds me to you, O God,
cannot be broken. It is like a diamond
that smashes the hammer when it is struck.

— Mira Bai

Mira Bai, a sixteenth-century Hindu devotee of Krishna, waxes eloquently of her love for God in the form of the *avatara,* or the Divine Incarnation of Krishna. This Divine Love that exists between God and the soul is eternal and cannot be destroyed. It is also unbreakable for another reason: The Divine Lover never withdraws his love once committed to us. She likens this two-way love to the extraordinary durability of a diamond that even a hammer cannot crack. Anything that would attempt to interpose itself between God and each one of us would similarly be smashed or overcome by the strength of that Divine Love. In all things, let us commit ourselves to God's love — his for us, and ours for him — and surrender to him in the various corners of our life.

[70]

Mystery is as important as information,
depth of emotion is as important as rational thinking,
and spiritual awakening is as important
as worldly pleasure.

— Russill Paul

My friend Russill Paul, an extraordinary musician, spiritual teacher, and author, reminds us in this passage from *The Yoga of Sound* how much we need to clarify our priorities. If we leave essential elements out of our lives, our inner experience becomes impoverished. If we emphasize only information, rational thought, and pleasure, our journey here will not be completed by meaning, direction, and belonging. Everywhere mystery surrounds us: our birth, childhood, relationships, significant experiences, old age, illness, death, and what is beyond. Likewise, emotional depth is a higher form of intelligence than mere rational understanding. It allows us to see and feel beyond what we know or think we know with mere reason. Finally, spiritual awakening, knowing the Divine, fulfills our purpose for being here. All three will always be more important than worldly pleasures, which pass away.

[71]

All mystical teaching that reveals the Divine Ground of human nature must face the paradox of our blindness to the Divine or our sense of alienation from the Divine. Human suffering and conflict are created by ignoring our rootedness in the Divine Ground.

— Lex Hixon

As Sufi Lex Hixon says in *Coming Home,* most of the human world distracts us from working toward our spiritual realization. Our spiritual and moral blindness account for our sense of separation or alienation from God, the basis of all our serious problems and suffering. When we ignore, obscure, or simply fail to realize our intrinsic relationship with the Divine, then in a very real sense we are uprooted from the soil of our being in the Divine Nature itself. We cannot long exist in this state of estrangement from God, however we define the Divine Source, even if it is simply an awareness of deeper meaning in our life. Without this life-giving relationship, people wither and die.

Virtue never stands alone.
It is bound to have neighbors.

— Confucius

China's great sage Confucius was celebrated for his oracular wisdom, which he often expressed aphoristically, particularly in The Analects, one of his major writings. Confucius placed a great deal of emphasis on virtue, and here he identifies one of its more practical advantages: that the virtuous man or woman attracts other people of virtue. The virtuous always seek out those who have attained this morally vibrant consciousness, for this company stimulates and reinforces their own commitment. The Indian tradition, both Hindu and Buddhist, counsels us to seek the company of the wise, to associate with people who have a similar conviction, who are looking in the same direction. One virtue usually implies others: A generous soul may also be courageous, kind, compassionate, loving, and patient. Mutual reinforcement is inevitable.

[73]

Happiness accompanies a virtuous life.

— Aristotle

⌒

Most people regard happiness as an end in itself, and in a certain sense it is. It is the ultimate destiny of this life's course. The Dalai Lama stresses that what we all have in common, regardless of our religious traditions, is that every one of us wants to be happy. It is a universal concern of all sentient beings. In his work on ethics, Aristotle, the Greek philosopher, elaborates on the importance of virtue and living virtuously. For him, and for many who shared his culture, a high point in the ancient world, happiness was only possible as a consequence of virtue. Far from an end in itself, it is the gift of commitment to the transformative values of moral consciousness, where these values become habits of thinking, speaking, and acting. Happiness is the reward of virtue, and seeking virtue will lead to happiness more surely than the singular pursuit of happiness. Let us focus on moral intelligence, as manifested in virtue, as our pursuit in life.

[74]

*We come from Joy; we are sustained in Joy,
and to Joy we will return.*

— The Upanishads

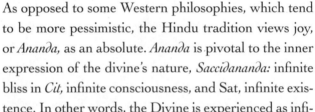

As opposed to some Western philosophies, which tend to be more pessimistic, the Hindu tradition views joy, or *Ananda,* as an absolute. *Ananda* is pivotal to the inner expression of the divine's nature, *Saccidananda:* infinite bliss in *Cit,* infinite consciousness, and Sat, infinite existence. In other words, the Divine is experienced as infinite joy, the total affirmation of being, and the inherent goodness of the Source. We arise in this radiant joy, and it surrounds us on every side in all of our living moments. At the end of our lives, we will unite with this joy, this bliss, forever. Such a vision gives us an absolute perspective, helping us to lead our lives in similar joy, understanding, and peace. Seek this joy in all the areas of your life and discern its presence everywhere.

[75]

*A certain participation in happiness can be had
in this life, but perfect and true happiness cannot
be had in this life. Joy is full when there remains
nothing to be desired.*

— St. Thomas Aquinas

St. Thomas Aquinas, the great Catholic theologian and philosopher of the thirteenth century, explored happiness in the light of eternity. Like the Buddha, he viewed all earthly happiness as imperfect and transitory. He saw "perfect and true happiness" as everlasting, the happiness enjoyed in the beatific vision, the vision of God in Paradise. Beatitude in this ultimate sense constitutes true happiness. Our life in this world is impermanent; it does not allow for the perfection of happiness. Joy cannot achieve satiation here because we are never fully satisfied when our desires are fulfilled. They always ring hollow at their core, and we always desire more. The perfection of happiness is when we know that joy of fullness that does not end. In this existence, we can only have a participated, or limited, happiness. May our joy journey to the realm of that fullness found in the vision of the Divine One.

How I long to see among dawn flowers
the face of God.

— Basho

⌒

Basho (1644–94), the Japanese poet and master of the haiku, extols the life of contemplation in the natural world, even as he sees the fleeting nature of mystical experience. In this brief wisp of verse, he conveys a deep longing for the Divine. Even as we feel his longing, this seed of realization shows that we can discover the Divine Presence in nature, in other sentient beings, in the depths of ourselves. The poet's sensitivity sees God's face in flowers, mountains, rivers, clouds, forests, the ocean. The longing to make tangible contact with the Source is a perennial human desire, and for some, a passion for the infinite, as Kierkegaard put it. This longing is a holy thing, a compass pointing us in the direction of the eternal and the fullness of life, the completion of our dreams.

The fact that our task is exactly as large as
our life makes it appear infinite.

— Franz Kafka

In this brief saying, Franz Kafka (1883–1924), the Czechoslovakian novelist and existentialist, explores what he regards as our task. His observation reminds me of an old saying in the Christian tradition that considers the heavy tasks God gives us: "The Lord fits the back for the burden." We are limited by our human perception, yet we remain responsible in shaping our being and becoming what we feel we've been called to become. In this matter, we have great freedom. Our task is co-extensive with our lives and so appears to us as endless or infinite. The purpose each one of us has is not merely a mission external to us, but has a lot to do with unfolding and developing our gifts, especially who we are in our capacity for mercy, kindness, and love, the cultivation of which is an essential part of the task of life. Let each of us have the courage to embrace our task.

We all need a certain amount of fallow time....
Watching the grass grow, sitting on the hillside,
staring out the window daydreaming. When we don't
have it, there is a deeper intelligence that won't come forth.

— Sue Bender

Enjoying "fallow" time gives scope to the imagination and the workings of grace inside of us. The urgency of the call to just be, in the present moment — the now — is eloquently given voice here by writer Sue Bender, author of *Everyday Sacred*. Bender was particularly drawn to the simplicity of lifestyle cultivated by the Amish, who provide a powerful counterpoint to our frantic days. We all regularly require free time to let go of control, yet we seem to find less and less of it. The deeper intelligence at work in all things eludes us when we fail to take time to be aware. Some may like to sit in a garden or on a front porch, others to take a walk through the forest or ride along a bike path, and still others to watch the stars or the ebb and flow of the ocean. We are contemplative beings, so make a resolution now to devote time to just being.

Monasticism of the heart
is the heart of monasticism.
— Brother David Steindl-Rast

This Austrian-born Benedictine monk, who is a very gifted contemplative, speaks to us about the essence of the monastic experience: the inner commitment to seek the Divine Presence. What makes a monk or a nun is the inner attitude of commitment to a life of prayer, not the outer trappings that help the monastic on his or her path. If a contemplative is not inwardly focused on the mystical life, then he or she is not following the perennial quest of monastic life: to seek God above all things. This inner commitment defines monastic life in its wellspring. As I wrote in *A Monk in the World*, it is increasingly common to pursue the life of a monk or a nun in the world. In that environment of busyness and time constraints, the heart's monasticism becomes completely essential. It is what nourishes the motivation, inspires the journey, and brings fruit in relationship to others. Let us all work in that monastery within, so that we can share its fruits without.

[80]

You are the clear space of awareness, pure and still,
in whom there is no birth, no activity, no "I."
You are the same. You cannot change or die.

— *The Heart of Awareness,*
a translation of the Ashtavakra Gita, by Thomas Byrom

Thomas Byrom's wonderful translation, *The Heart of Awareness,* makes available to us one of the ancient spiritual treasures of the *Advaita Vedanta* tradition of Hindu contemplative life. Advaita is the experience and consciousness of nonduality, of a unified awareness that defines each one of our actual abiding natures and identities. *Advaita Vedanta* is one of the dominant streams of the Indian mystical and philosophical tradition. Each one of us has always been in the pure root of identity as awareness and consciousness, free of a limited self, of a phenomenal ego or false self. Through meditation, we discover this ultimate, limitless ground of identity in pure awareness. This is the true self, the eternal being that cannot be born and cannot die. The egoistic identity is impermanent, but the abiding awareness of the self is everlasting.

[81]

Consciousness is the Self of which everyone is aware.
No one is ever away from his Self
and therefore everyone is in fact Self-realized.
Only...people don't know this and want to realize the Self.

— Sri Ramana Maharshi

Ramana Maharshi, a modern Indian mystic saint of the twentieth century, presents here a classic *Advaitic* understanding: Consciousness is who we really are. The secret of our identity is hidden within its mystery; it conveys our identity. Indeed, it is the very act of being aware that is the self. Awareness is the soul; awareness is the permanent identity; awareness continues throughout life, all time, and eternity. It is so close to us and so obvious that many miss it. Consciousness is self-realized in being aware. Nothing happens outside of awareness, for all reality requires consciousness to be. Consciousness is immaterial and thus totally indestructible. It is spirit, the eternal self.

Dialogue must begin, first of all, within oneself.
If we cannot make peace within, how can we hope
to bring about peace in the world?

— Thich Nhat Hanh

This saintly Vietnamese Zen monk expresses a fundamental truth about the process of peace-making in the
world: it begins within our own thought processes. This
may seem simple, but it is not. This notion, the foundation of modern psychology and the therapeutic process,
holds the single key to world peace that supersedes
our negotiations, summits, and governmental policies.
External peace-making requires internal clarity, determination, and continued vigilance. The internal dialogue requires us to be very clear about where we stand
personally, to be certain that our commitment to nonviolence is absolute. It demands of us to be continually
vigilant over our thoughts, emotions, and reactions.
Held in the flux of our emotional reactions — now
peaceful, then violent, then peaceful again — we lack
the inward stability to convey any genuine *outward*
peace. Only with emotional stability and awareness do
we become effective instruments of peace.

All is emptiness and all is compassion.

— Buddha

This aphorism attributed to the Buddha sums up the teaching of Buddhist *Dharma*. It is the realization of everyone who awakens, no matter the tradition to which they belong and the language in which it is expressed. Before one can understand through intense awareness that compassion is the point of life in our relationships with all beings, one must first understand the nature of reality: emptiness. With the exception of the Eternal Foundation of Consciousness, everything is impermanent, passing away, in constant flux. Because everything is constantly changing, nothing actually exists on its own. Each one of us is dependent on others and nature to be. Everything is interdependent. When we grasp inwardly the truth of impermanence, then we also understand that all is compassion, for then we know that we are intrinsically and fundamentally related to everyone and everything else.

[84]

I AM WHO I AM.

— Exodus 3:14

These extraordinarily powerful words of *Yahweh* were uttered to Moses on Mount Sinai. The blazing, over-powering realization they transmit is that only God is real in the ultimate sense. He is the one who truly is; all else derives from him because nothing else exists in this unique way. The Divine is existence itself, whereas we have existence from him. God's revelation of his name also signifies that he is the one who causes all to be. God, or *Yahweh,* is also the one who is truly present and is the Presence itself. This profound statement is at once a metaphysical truth and a spiritual orientation in our mystical journey: the goal of the earthly sojourn before us.

[85]

The soul is kissed by God in its innermost regions.

— Hildegard of Bingen

We are made for intimacy with the Divine. God communicates his being to us in the grace of love within the depths of spirit that each one of us is. Because we are made for God, for undying joy, only he can fulfill each one of us. God's kiss transmits the grace of his presence and makes our transformation possible. His kiss is a promise of and an invitation to divine union in mystical intimacy. The innermost regions of which the twelfth-century mystic Hildegard speaks refer to the soul spark, the fine point of the spirit, that uncreated and uncreatable essence that each one of us has. The Divine kiss as promise and invitation requires a response from us, and our response is the substance of life's purpose. That we may have the generosity and wisdom to respond.

[86]

We come from Love; we are sustained in Love,
and to Love we shall return.

— Christian saying

This aphorism sums up the Christian understanding of life. It parallels the Hindu statement on joy or *Ananda* as the source and destiny of human life. The New Testament writers make it very clear that God is love, a phrase they mean quite literally. That doesn't mean that human love is God, but that the Divine Essence has infinite concern, compassion, kindness, mercy, and sensitivity for *us*. This love has an infinite number of dimensions, and each dimension is itself endless. The Divine Reality is not a cold philosophical, analytical intelligence, though it is pure intelligence also, but a warm radiance of light. We arise eternally in this love; it maintains us in being, nourishing us in each moment; and it is our final destiny to be united to this love forever.

[87]

The ultimate work of civilization is the unfolding
of ever-deeper spiritual understanding.

— Arnold Toynbee

The great British historian Arnold Toynbee offers this take on history, which he has arrived at after a lifetime of study. The notion of spirit plays an operative role in the development of civilizations, in the structure of culture, religion, art, poetry, science, music, literature, law, and government. All the great civilizations have made some progress in revealing the spiritual reality of life and the purpose of human experience in this world. We are, however, very far from where we should be. Our understanding must know much more substantial and ecumenical growth, a growth that spreads its arms to embrace all the great notions put forth by the human family, with its multitudes of religions and spiritualities. The "unfolding of spiritual understanding" refers not just to spiritual growth, but to spiritual synthesis, a bringing together of the great, life-affirming traditions. This is not an easy task, and it becomes more difficult in this period of division and conflict. May we all do our part to bring about this global transformation.

[88]

*Until humankind extends its circle of compassion
to all living things, it will not itself find peace.*

— Albert Schweitzer

Humanitarian and theologian Dr. Albert Schweitzer's truth recognizes the inherent right of all living beings to exist unmolested by the human community, an understanding that thankfully continues to grow. His view rests on a mature understanding of *ahimsa,* or nonharming, and what he came to articulate as reverence for *all* life. Schweitzer, who died in 1965, was undoubtedly far ahead of his time. Learning this compassion and extending the circle to embrace all living beings requires considerable awareness, but it is attainable by those who are alert to both its necessity and its possibility. This development and attainment means that we must allow life to stretch us beyond the assumptions of our early conditioning and cultural education so that we can come to a higher understanding of life. That we may embrace our animal brethren, recognizing our common bonds and needs, and find the peace we all seek.

[89]

*I claim to be a simple individual liable to err
like any other fellow mortal.
I own, however, that I have humility enough
to confess my errors and to retrace my steps.*

— Mahatma Gandhi

There is no possibility of a mature spiritual life without humility. Nor is it possible to be a successful human being without it. Humility is also, most fundamentally, a relationship of truth with ourselves. Humility begins with self-honesty about our actions, attitudes, and speech. It compels us to accept the fact that we are capable of being wrong, perhaps even when we are convinced we are right. It means that we acknowledge our mistakes, not years from now, but when they are made. We must be willing to own up to these mistakes before others and not simply ourselves. Such humility is a basic operating principle of ordinary life. Without it, we can hardly move at all, since the mystical process is based on honesty and humility of heart. Search your experience and examine if humility is at work in you.

The friend is the key and I am the lock.

— Rumi

Rumi uncovers for us here a secret way into the bliss of the Divine Presence: the precious gift of spiritual friendship. The spiritual friend is not just a friend whose company we enjoy. Such friendships are important and nourishing to us in some necessary way, but they don't touch our depth of being. Friendship in its mystical significance is always a relationship in the light of eternity; it is a bond related to our eternal mutual well-being. Although it partakes of all the joys of affection normal among friends, it has its origin and destiny in the Divine itself. The friend, in this sense, is a mirror for us, and we are a mirror for them. This friend is someone with whom we can share our deepest thoughts and fears, someone who inspires us, reminds us, and corrects us when we need it. Such friends share prayer, meditation, and reflection with us, and all the joys that arise in the mystical journey. These rare friendships are the highest form of love there is after Divine Love itself.

[91]

May the Lord increase and make abundant
the love you have for one another, and towards all persons…
to the end that God may establish your hearts
blameless in holiness.

— 1 Thessalonians 3:11–13

Here St. Paul expresses his deepest prayer for the Christian community of Thessalonia: that its members may know the blessings of Divine Love's radiance in their lives and know its inexhaustible abundance, and that it will grow in them, reaching perfection in the One itself. This love must not be hoarded and confined to our little circle of family and friends, but increased, reaching out to all of our encounters and relationships. In this way it becomes as abundant as the Source itself, transforming our hearts and making us holy and blameless in God's presence. Holiness permeates our entire being: our thoughts, intentions, will, unconscious life, dreams, and actions. Surrender then to Divine Love in your life and experience its transformation of your being.

The principle of the one who experiences
the inner life is to become all things to all
people. In every situation, in every capacity,
he answers the demand of the moment.

— Hazrat Inayat Khan

Hazrat Inayat Khan, the great Islamic mystic sage and founder of the Sufi Order of the West, directs our attention to a principle that St. Paul also followed in his time. The inner life calls us into the integrity of the present moment, the now; it demands of us a mindfulness. In compassion, kindness, and love, we discern what is needed and we respond. We are a good listener to some, a provider of strength to others, a fierce advocate and prophet to still others. To many we are teachers, and we strive to understand the backgrounds, faiths, and experiences of everyone and especially to commiserate with their suffering and wounds. We do not need to compromise who we are, rather to understand what is needed in each situation and become a sign of hope, clarity, and love to others. This ability is a gift of the Divine.

[93]

They have realized the goal who realize Brahman
as the supreme reality, the source of truth, wisdom,
and boundless joy. They see the Lord in the cave of the heart
and are granted all the blessings of life.

— Taittiriya Upanishad

The Hindu and Buddhist traditions place great emphasis
on the importance of realization. For them, the word *realization* has a special meaning quite different from its use
and connotation in the West, where it refers to understanding something or experiencing a breakthrough.
Where the West views it on the level of thought, realization in the East is far more experiential and existential. As
told here in the Taittiriya Upanishad, one of the chapters
of the Yajur Veda, to realize Brahman, the Godhead and
Source of all that is, is to experience the Source directly,
to be united to the Divine without mediation. This quality of realization the Indian tradition calls *brahmavidya,*
the mystical awakening to the overpowering integration
with God. This mystical breakthrough happens within
the depths of subjectivity, what India calls the *guha,* the
cave of the heart. This experience is the goal of Indian
mysticism; it points the way to *moksha,* or liberation from
the cycle of rebirth. Each one of us must endeavor to
make this same realization. May it be so.

What is essential is invisible to the eyes.

— Bolivian proverb

When we look with our eyes, we perceive only a tiny fraction of what is. So much of reality is beyond the scope of our grasping minds, transcending our ability to conceive it. The essential reality is the mystical dimension, the order related to Divinity. The essential also includes the deep stirrings of the heart, the unconscious mind, and the emotions. All these aspects of reality are hidden and not easily understood without effort. During the course of our spiritual journey, we must develop some clarity about these realities and especially how they take shape in our lives. May we each become attuned to the essential reality that is invisible.

*Just as the mind digests ideas and produces intelligence,
the soul feeds on life and digests it, creating wisdom and
character out of the fodder of experience.*

— Thomas Moore

In his wonderful book *The Care of the Soul,* Thomas
Moore uncovers something of how the soul and mind
operate and are nourished by the experiences of life.
The mind absorbs ideas, many of which are connected
with impressions of objects in the world. Then the intellect fashions them and puts them into use in the
realm of intelligence. Intelligence is constantly making
sense of the world through the ideas the mind enter-
tains. A cohesive system of ideas produces the intelligence with which we understand everything around
us. The soul operates in a similar manner. The soul is
always imbibing reality, learning from all the experience it is given. Then the soul "translates" this experience into wisdom, an experiential knowing that
informs and develops a consistent response to life —
what we call character.

[96]

To know the Tao is to still the mind.
Knowledge comes with perseverance.

— Loy Ching Yuen,
Taoist master

⌒

Taoism says that stillness is the greatest revelation. Here we see more specific advice that suggests a method for experiencing the Tao, the Divine. When we enter meditation through awareness of the stillness, we discover God directly. This requires us to quiet the mind, a very difficult exercise that comes with practice. When we are inwardly quiet in our thoughts and desires, we become aware of the inner stillness. The Tao is present in this quiet, this inner stillness beyond the mind. As we dwell with the Tao in this silence, we grow in the knowledge of the Tao and our wisdom about the nature of life. Work to be with the stillness, incorporate openness to the stillness in your meditation, and finally extend it to the mind. See what happens!

*Compassion is the keen awareness
of the interdependence of all things.*

— Thomas Merton

⌒

Thomas Merton, the great Trappist monk and contemplative, learned a lot from other traditions, grappling with his own faith to incorporate the wisdom of others. From Buddhism he learned about interdependence, though this insight is present in all the great world religions, including Christianity. Buddhism, however, made interdependence a priority in its view of existence. When we grasp the eternal truth of interdependence, a natural or spontaneous compassion arises for all beings. The apprehension of the intrinsic interconnectedness of all leads organically to a compassion for all, especially in the concrete existential situations of life as we meet others each day. Simply put, when we realize we are all in this together, our kindness and understanding grows. We are all related; we are all responsible for one another.

[98]

No person was ever honored for what he received.
Honor has been the reward for what he gave.

— Calvin Coolidge

What Calvin Coolidge claims in the secular context of
service certainly holds true as a spiritual principle as
well. One authentic form of happiness comes from giving — giving that is motivated by the simple joy of
doing it. And as those who make giving a life habit will
tell you, rewards come in unexpected forms. Each one
of us also needs to locate the giving identity of service
within and live out its truth in all our attempts to aid
others.

[99]

A teacher affects eternity;
he can never tell where his influence stops.

— Henry Adams

As a teacher, I can appreciate this hopeful bit of wisdom from Henry Adams (1838–1918), a grandson and great-grandson of American presidents who eschewed politics to travel, write, learn, and observe the world. The enormous influence teachers exert on the lives of their students, as Adams observes, "affects eternity." My Uncle John, who was a great teacher, used to say: "Our students are precious beings. We must guard them with special care." We all have teachers who changed the paths of our lives. It is not for teachers to look for what that influence is or will be; it is enough that they know they have served the needs of these tender souls, leaving the rest to the Divine.

Flow with whatever may happen and let your mind be free.
Stay centered by accepting whatever you are doing.
This is the ultimate.

— Chuang Tzu

Chuang Tzu, one of the early sources of Taoist mysticism, offers us a method for acting, creating, and being. The Tao is always a flow of being. As you flow with the moment, the mind should be detached, unhindered by what it identifies as good or bad events. Whatever presents itself to your experience, accept it. Be open to what is. By entering into the flow with freedom and acceptance, you are in a position to respond as necessary. At the same time, this approach allows us to harness our greatest creativity. Give yourself permission to embrace the flow of each moment, with an attitude of inner freedom and acceptance of what is before you.

[101]

In him we live and move and have our being.

— Acts 17:28

⌒

This profound statement from the Acts of the Apostles is a central teaching in the New Testament. All things, including us — *especially* us — are within God's consciousness. Nothing exists outside this all-encompassing awareness. We exist in God; we move, grow, understand, and act within Divine Awareness. This insight is radical and powerful. It grants us perspective, the strength to follow the course of our lives in its ultimacy.

[102]

After the age of thirty, all psychological problems
are spiritual in nature.

— Carl Jung

Carl Jung, widely known as a student of Freud, actually rescued psychiatry and psychology from the clutches of Freudian atheism. Jung was a significant pioneer in the study of the unconscious, dreams, and symbolism. He discovered the archetypes of the unconscious, the collective images and meanings universally present in everyone and often accessed through dream states. Jung understood the nature of the healthy psyche and how much it requires a sense of the Divine. He came to realize through his practice that the root of each problem was a spiritual cause related to a sense of separation from God. He came to see how this sense of separation fuels illness. Jung thus grasped the close proximity of psychology to spirituality. He saw that we need spiritual wisdom as the healing source for pathological states.

The Holy Spirit flows through us with the
marvelous creative power of everlasting joy.
— Mechthild of Magdeburg

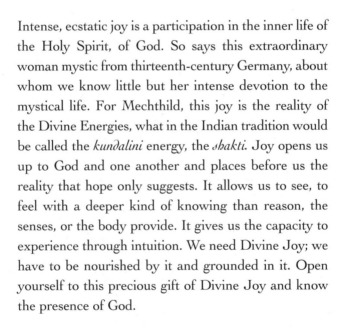

Intense, ecstatic joy is a participation in the inner life of the Holy Spirit, of God. So says this extraordinary woman mystic from thirteenth-century Germany, about whom we know little but her intense devotion to the mystical life. For Mechthild, this joy is the reality of the Divine Energies, what in the Indian tradition would be called the *kundalini* energy, the *shakti*. Joy opens us up to God and one another and places before us the reality that hope only suggests. It allows us to see, to feel with a deeper kind of knowing than reason, the senses, or the body provide. It gives us the capacity to experience through intuition. We need Divine Joy; we have to be nourished by it and grounded in it. Open yourself to this precious gift of Divine Joy and know the presence of God.

Fear is the mind-killer. I will not give in to it.

— Frank Herbert

⁓

The great science fiction writer Frank Herbert filled his *Dune* series with considerable spiritual wisdom. The above saying comes from the Bene Gesserit teaching from the Litany Against Fear, which appears throughout Frank Herbert's eight volumes of *Dune*. It is an effective way to overcome one's fears in this life, especially in this dark period of history we find ourselves in. The Bene Gesserit sisters would recite the fairly long Litany Against Fear whenever confronted with danger. The power of words, like a mantra, can help us fight fear's effect of paralyzing us into inaction and silencing us when we should be a witness to the truth. We need to guard ourselves against fear's deadening effect. We must cast it aside. Behind every fear is our terror of death, the great unknown. Let us see through our fears and relinquish them to what is possible beyond them. Allow your fear to be deflated by your hope and your unwillingness to be crippled by its hold.

[105]

Before the Unconditioned, the conditioned dances:
"Thou and I are one!" this trumpet proclaims.

— Kabir

⌒

This life is not separate from the eternal. Most of what we know in this existence pertains to the conditioned being we experience, but it is the Unconditioned Reality of the Divine that grounds our life in this realm. The conditioned existence can only be in relationship to the Divine, the Unconditioned itself. As Kabir, the mystic poet of India, tells us, the conditioned "dances" in the presence of the Conditioned. In the Divine, it lives, develops, and fulfills its purpose. Kabir exalts in this awareness and the realization that we are at home in the eternal. The Unconditioned, the Godhead, is our ultimate home, and we are all in transit to that reality. This realization, which dawns on every mystic, is the source of endless joy and ecstasy.

Genius is the ability to put into effect
what is in your mind.

— F. Scott Fitzgerald

An old friend of mine was fond of saying that "genius is the capacity for hard work." Maybe that's most of what the great novelist Fitzgerald meant, but creative genius seems a more mysterious process. Many more people can *recognize* great art than can *produce* it. We all hold a reverence for the beauty and inspiration that art produces in us. We may even have the creative spark to imagine a work of art ourselves. But the creative process is fraught with difficulties, and the act of creation is what matters. The drive and inspiration to pursue a talent, "to put into effect what is in your mind," the unrelenting perseverance to see it through to actuality — that is genius. We aren't all great novelists, but we all have a genius for something. Find what you have a talent for and pursue it into birth.

They change their sky, not their soul,

who run across the sea.

— Horace

The great Roman writer Horace shares with us a fundamental truth about human identity, the truth of being part of a nation, culture, or religious tradition. The bonds of nation, ethnicity, community, and tribe are deep. The lure of our native land, our childhood neighborhood, our home country, is magnetic and powerfully seductive. It holds us, inspires us, and calls to the romantic in each one of us. It is important for us to have a sense of connection with, and pride of, place. Yet at the same time, our passion and pride can spill over into bigotry, nationalism, and hatred. Holding our love and pride in balance with tolerance and openness is the task of citizens living in a globalized world.

When God crowns our merits
he crowns his own gifts.

— St. Augustine of Hippo

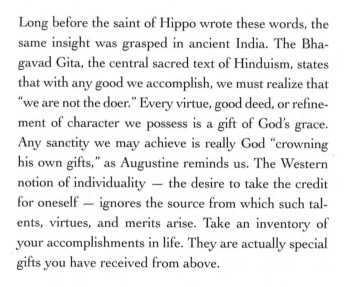

Long before the saint of Hippo wrote these words, the same insight was grasped in ancient India. The Bhagavad Gita, the central sacred text of Hinduism, states that with any good we accomplish, we must realize that "we are not the doer." Every virtue, good deed, or refinement of character we possess is a gift of God's grace. Any sanctity we may achieve is really God "crowning his own gifts," as Augustine reminds us. The Western notion of individuality — the desire to take the credit for oneself — ignores the source from which such talents, virtues, and merits arise. Take an inventory of your accomplishments in life. They are actually special gifts you have received from above.

[109]

*Friendship is a precious jewel,
so hard to find and so easily lost.*

— John Cosgrove

My beloved Uncle John was a very wise man. In addition to his depth of kindness and wit, he summed up moral teachings with his own little aphorisms. The one above on friendship was especially meaningful to me, and Uncle John never tired of uttering these words to me. Over the years I have come to understand profoundly how precious friendship actually is, how rare the true friend is with whom we can share important moments in our earthly journey.

[110]

Innocence is not a symbol — it is a fact.
It is only the innocent mind that can see clearly,
that can see something new.

— J. Krishnamurti

⌒

Like Shunryu Suzuki's Zen notion of "beginner's mind," Krishnamurti emphasized the spiritual importance of innocence. We can discern true innocence in children, animals, and our own remembrance of childhood, as well as in simple faith. Innocence is openness and wonder. It is not hard-hearted, but free. It has no vested interests, but is always experiencing everything as new, refreshing, and exciting. The innocent mind remains clear and curious. Luckily, innocence can be regained by cultivating an attitude of openness and a nonmanipulative relationship with others, our work, and ourselves. Meditation also helps to regain innocence, keeping the mind and heart receptive, nongrasping, and loving. In this world of cynicism, seek innocence in the depths of your intention and hold fast to it.

My religion is kindness.

— The Dalai Lama

An eager reporter once asked the Dalai Lama what he believed. The journalist was really trying to find out what made His Holiness tick. The Dalai Lama was not put off by his question, but saw it was motivated by a sincere curiosity about a person few actually understand. His Holiness smiled at the man and with great gentleness and love said, "It's really quite simple. My religion is kindness!" Here he put his finger on one of the genuine fruits of spirituality. Christians, Jews, Muslims, and Hindus can also say, "My religion is kindness and love." Let us each examine our faith. If it is rooted in love, mercy, kindness, and compassion, we are on the right track.

*I thank God for my handicaps, for through them
I have found myself, my work, and my God.*

— Helen Keller

Born blind and deaf, Helen Keller had no way to communicate with the outside world that surrounded her. Because someone believed in her, she learned to read Braille and to speak effectively. She became a champion of many causes, but especially of the deaf and the blind. Few who have all their faculties and senses can accomplish even a fraction of what Helen Keller did. What appeared as obstacles in her way turned out to be the means of self-discovery, mastery, and growth of her faith, which bore fruit in an intensely satisfying relationship with God. Seeing our shortcomings, challenges, and setbacks as blessings certainly requires a robust perspective. But oftentimes, that is truly what they are. Nothing is impossible to someone with the determination to translate obstacles into victories. Those obstacles are often precisely what lend us the strength and the wisdom to face life anew.

Progress is impossible without change; and those who cannot change their minds cannot change anything.

— George Bernard Shaw

Change is often painful and difficult. The older we get, the more we resist change and view it as a threat. Most people cling to the security of the familiar. When the Roman Catholic Church, for instance, called the Second Vatican Council, it generated far-reaching change in ecclesial life, discipline, and liturgy. It abandoned Latin and adopted the vernacular of each country as the official language of the Church and radically changed the Church's relationship with other traditions. These changes were too much for millions of Catholics, who left the Church. Change takes an open mind and heart; it requires courage and vision, as well as imagination and hope in the future. What is your attitude toward change? Are your mind and heart open?

[114]

Attend to the grand allowing!

— Martha Bartholomew,
mystic and spiritual teacher

The "allowing" of the above exhortation refers to openness and receptivity of mind and heart before the great mystery of life that progressively unfolds for us. We must say yes to it with our whole being. The grand allowing is powered by spirit and is the work of grace within us. The Divine suggests new approaches, attitudes, and ways of being in the course of our lives. Our task is to allow, to let be, to become, and this often means moving beyond the secure into places of vulnerability. Such movement is challenging but also rewarding. Attending to the grand allowing, we are positioned for quantum leaps of growth, an evolution into higher and more subtle states of mind and heart. That we may each say yes to this grand allowing and surrender to being.

O Love that loves me more than I can
love myself or understand.

— St. Teresa of Avila

⌒

Teresa of Avila was given the extraordinary gift of union with God. She was granted God's love to an ultimate degree, to the point that she uttered these words. This Divine Love is incomprehensible to us, because it so overflows our capacity to love and so to understand it. We humans have an infinite capacity for love but only a finite experience. When we are given awareness of God's love for us, all we can do is receive its power in awe and respond to it with as much love as we are capable. Human beings — for most of their lives — only know this love through faith, conviction, theological speculation, or guesses. In mystical experience, we know it directly, and it changes us forever.

*Meditation is the creative control of the self
where the Infinite can talk to you.*

— Yogi Bhajan

Yogi Bhajan is an American Sikh spiritual leader and a well-known master of yoga and meditation. "Creative control of the self" means control of the body but more importantly the control of the processes of thought. Usually thought has control over the self. If we can give up our thoughts in meditation, we can give up the ego that binds us to the limited reality we know in everyday life. When the self is purified through the meditative process, it is freed to converse with the Infinite One. It is up to each one of us to choose this ultimate good and give ourselves to the Ultimate. Plunge into the bliss of the Infinite One who waits for you eternally in a peace beyond your understanding.

[117]

*I have but one lamp by which my feet are guided,
and that is the lamp of experience.*

— Patrick Henry

There really is no substitute for experience. As early American patriot Patrick Henry, whose notion of individual rights and independence sparked the American revolution, put it so succinctly, experience is a sure guide, providing we have the wisdom to examine its lessons. Direct experience is the best teacher, especially along the spiritual journey. We can read about mystical experience, but until we are confronted with its overwhelming primacy, mystical experience is just words. Do you trust your experience? What else do we have?

[118]

Whatever a person sows
that also he shall reap.

— Galatians 6:8

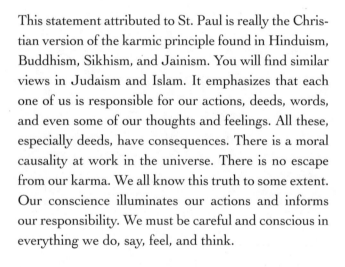

This statement attributed to St. Paul is really the Christian version of the karmic principle found in Hinduism, Buddhism, Sikhism, and Jainism. You will find similar views in Judaism and Islam. It emphasizes that each one of us is responsible for our actions, deeds, words, and even some of our thoughts and feelings. All these, especially deeds, have consequences. There is a moral causality at work in the universe. There is no escape from our karma. We all know this truth to some extent. Our conscience illuminates our actions and informs our responsibility. We must be careful and conscious in everything we do, say, feel, and think.

All those who live by the sword
shall die by the sword.

— Gospel of Matthew 26:52

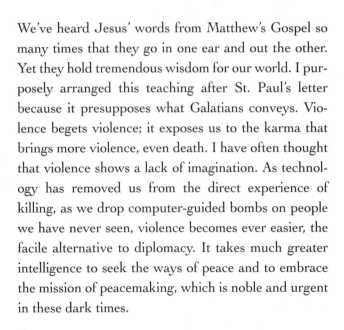

We've heard Jesus' words from Matthew's Gospel so many times that they go in one ear and out the other. Yet they hold tremendous wisdom for our world. I purposely arranged this teaching after St. Paul's letter because it presupposes what Galatians conveys. Violence begets violence; it exposes us to the karma that brings more violence, even death. I have often thought that violence shows a lack of imagination. As technology has removed us from the direct experience of killing, as we drop computer-guided bombs on people we have never seen, violence becomes ever easier, the facile alternative to diplomacy. It takes much greater intelligence to seek the ways of peace and to embrace the mission of peacemaking, which is noble and urgent in these dark times.

If I am not for myself, who will be for me?
And if I am only for myself, what am I?
And if not now — when?

— Hillel the Elder

Hillel, a wise Jewish sage, identifies the delicate balance we must constantly walk, between a life in which we surrender needs and desires to the authority of others and a solipsistic existence in which we ignore the needs and desires of others. It takes wisdom, generosity, and a good heart to negotiate this balance. It doesn't come easy. We have to work at it and be constantly reminded, honestly examining ourselves periodically. Without self-respect, we'll never gain the respect of others. Yet those who are only for themselves aren't fully human; they've missed the point and work of life. Hillel also reminds us that we have to work at it now, not tomorrow, next week, or ten years from now. It's the task for each moment.

[121]

Happiness is a perfume you cannot pour on others without getting a few drops on yourself.

— Ralph Waldo Emerson

The poet, essayist, and American Transcendentalist Ralph Waldo Emerson understood something beautiful about the nature of happiness: It's meant to be shared. As the Buddhists say, individual happiness by itself, alone, is an illusion. It's superficial and doesn't last. When we work for the happiness of others, or as the poet says, pour it on others, we become happy in the process. Again, this insight is similar to what we discovered in Aristotle's notion of happiness as the accompaniment of virtue. What we give out returns to us, and if we are constantly contributing to the welfare, joy, and happiness of others, we will receive these blessings in return. Are you pouring drops of happiness on others?

And the person who, at the last hour, remembers Me only,
departs leaving the body, enters into Me;
of that there is no doubt.

— Bhagavad Gita

The Bhagavad Gita is the crystallization of the Hindu tradition, a compendium of all the streams of wisdom found in the Sanatana Dharma. All the discoveries India has made about mystical reality are contained in this compelling sacred text: the transcendent One, the immanent self, the yogic path, *advaita* or the focus on nondual awareness. But the most consistent teaching of the Gita is its personalism, so dramatically expressed in the dialogue between the protagonists: Lord Krishna, an incarnation of the god Vishnu, and Arjuna. The above passage emphasizes the single-minded focus on God that leads to union with him. The theme followed here is remembrance of the Divine. The Gita tells us emphatically that Divine beatitude awaits anyone who cultivates this remembrance of God.

Purity of heart is to will one thing.

— Søren Kierkegaard

This adage of Kierkegaard's — after which he named an entire book — is similar in meaning to the preceding quotation from the Bhagavad Gita. The melancholy Danish philosopher was a very committed Christian, and in this observation on the nature of pure intention, he emphasized the dedication we all need in our spiritual lives, in our relationships with the Source, the Divine Lover who is always beckoning us toward him. Kierkegaard points in the direction of where transformation and salvation are to be found. Transformation and salvation are not part-time matters; they ask of us a total commitment over a lifetime.

[124]

Pluck out self-love as you would a faded lotus flower.

— The Dhammapada

In the West, we spend a lot of time encouraging people to love and cherish themselves. Presumably we are trying to combat the seeming epidemic of low self-esteem and self-hate. Once, during a luncheon in New Mexico, His Holiness the Dalai Lama asked Father Thomas Keating and me why it was that so many Americans had such low self-esteem. I'm not sure I have the answer, although I think the mass media might be partially to blame. But the Dhammapada, a sacred Buddhist text, is not referring to people who lack self-acceptance but to the other side of the coin of human frailty — unhealthy self-absorption. "Self-love," as the Buddha calls it, is an obstacle to true awareness, another impediment along the spiritual journey.

[125]

To love what you do and feel that it matters —
how could anything be more fun?

— Katherine Graham

The late owner of the *Washington Post* Katherine Graham expresses the ideal work life: to be passionate about a talent you have and discover that you can make a career out of it. Work then becomes play instead of drudgery. But she makes another distinction often lost in our discussions of career choices. It is not enough to love your work. It also has to matter. Your job should be meaningful and beneficial to others, both to individuals and to the larger society in some way. Most people perform loveless jobs in order to survive; their work is neither fun nor fulfilling. Although they are unhappy, they plod along, never considering the possibility of enjoying a meaningful career. Perhaps our society should reconsider its priorities. Not everyone will enjoy his job, but creating more work that helps people, rather than work that simply creates profit for shareholders, might go a long way toward creating more meaningful jobs. Do you enjoy your job? Is it meaningful? What steps are you willing to take to secure a career that would really inspire you and others?

[126]

Always keep everything in perspective.

— Sister Mary Roman

Although this is good advice for any situation, Sister Mary Roman, a Carmelite nun and wonderful friend of mine, gave me this bit of advice about entering the monastic life. "Do you have any advice for me as I embark on this journey?" I asked her. "Very little in life is worth getting disturbed about," she replied. "Always keep everything in perspective." We human beings have a propensity to react and often overreact to virtually anything that happens. Yet most things are not worth getting upset over. To follow this advice means that we have to be patient and let most things go. We will know what we should respond to, what calls for real action and what does not. It takes maturity, clarity, and insight, but if we calm ourselves and listen to our inner intuition, we will know the difference.

[127]

The first step in personhood
is to allow ourselves to be loved.

— John Main

When we accept love from others, we open ourselves to the possibility of genuine happiness, which arises in us as we find ourselves giving love in return. Being loved increases our own capacities to love — to be merciful, kind, compassionate, and sensitive — all capacities that lead to true happiness. Love opens up the whole spectrum of human greatness: other-centeredness, self-sacrifice, heroic virtue, joy, and deeds of extraordinary generosity.

When you begin to touch your heart or let your heart
be touched, you begin to discover that it is bottomless,
that it doesn't have any resolution, that this heart is huge,
vast and limitless. You begin to discover how much warmth
and gentleness is there, as well as how much space.

— Pema Chödrön

Pema Chödrön, a Tibetan Buddhist teacher from Nova
Scotia, here presents a classical Tibetan teaching associated with the awakening to compassion. When we allow
ourselves to be open, to feel our vulnerability, to be
affected by others and reality itself, and when we can
know deeply what is real in our feelings, we realize that
our capacities for kindness, gentleness, and loving are endless. We have, and are, what the Tibetans call the "good
heart," a center of intention, openness, virtue, and compassion, all of which have taken root in our being, motivation,
attitudes, and behavior. The spiritual life has a lot to do
with getting in touch with this capacity. Like the blue sky,
sometimes the focus of Tibetan meditation, the mind and
heart are endless in their ability to know or be aware
and to feel, especially care, concern, loving-kindness, and
compassion. Are you in touch with your heart's vast nature?
If not, find the way there. You are not far from yourself.

The only thing we have to fear is fear itself.

— Franklin D. Roosevelt

This often-repeated quote has lost much of its context since it was first uttered by President Roosevelt during World War II. No doubt the fear at that time was as great as any fear now. Roosevelt, a gifted orator, allayed the American people's fears at a time when there wasn't a lot of good news or much cause to hope. Roosevelt knew that fear was a psychological problem — that it had more to do with human doubt, uncertainties, and lack of clarity about the unknown than with real danger. Human fear functions much like the stock market: nothing really makes it rise or fall except our psychological states of confidence or fearfulness about whether it will rise or fall. Our fears come from a similar place of doubt, often with no objective reality behind them. Awareness is the answer.

[130]

*I believe that the first test of a truly great man
is his humility. I don't mean by humility, doubt of his
power. But really great people have a curious feeling
that the greatness is not of them but through them.
And they see something divine in every other person
and are endlessly, foolishly, incredibly merciful.*

— John Ruskin

Many great novelists talk about how their fiction comes
through them, that they are a conduit for the stories of
their characters, whose voices create dialogue and story
lines the author couldn't anticipate. For Victorian John
Ruskin, this is the essential source of humility. Humility,
as this great Russian writer points out, is the modesty one
develops about the nature of greatness and the mercy
one has toward others as a result. The humble know that
something larger is the doer in us, and so their hearts are
open to others. They are keenly aware that the Divine
flows through all of us and that any claim we have to
greatness actually belongs to God, who is the doer in us.
This is also a significant theme in the Bhagavad Gita of
the Hindu tradition. Humility springs from the truth
of the Divine Reality and the truth about ourselves.

[131]

*I am an optimist. It does not seem
too much use being anything else.*

— Winston Churchill

Surely a pessimist could not have led Britain through
the darkness of World War II. Perhaps Churchill
learned his optimism during this immense challenge to
his leadership. His quip, or should we say advice, inti-
mates that optimism is a choice. A future can be built
on optimism but not on its opposite. When people give
in to doubt or base their life on cynicism, it paralyzes
them; it shrinks their being, compresses their dreams,
and deflates their expectations. An optimist is someone
who knows that ultimately things have a way of working out. Optimism is a mystical quality, and possessing
this quality is very useful in leading the spiritual life.

The age of leaders has come and gone. You must be
your own leader now. You must contain the spirit of
our time in your own life and your own nature.

— Laurens van der Post

Twentieth-century writer Laurens van der Post, long
recognized as someone with great sensitivity to the wisdom of the cultures he has lived in and studied, presents
us with a curiously modern principle of self-leadership.
Self-leadership presupposes that the person is not on an
ego trip and that he/she is mature and other-centered.
Furthermore, it assumes the person so individually directed in the more enlightened sense is on the spiritual
journey. We have to stand on our own two feet in this
age because genuine leaders are rare, and we have to
trust our own inner wisdom. We have to have faith in
our own abilities to take us to a place of safety for
humanity and other sentient beings. A leader only shows
you what you truly have and are. Each one of us is capable of being a leader for ourselves and to carry within
us the spirit of our age. Inner leadership is really the call
of the mystic, and when we heed this call we are growing up — we are finding our way in an essential sense.
Take charge of becoming your own leader.

[133]

The heart has reasons that reason knows nothing about.

— Blaise Pascal

Blaise Pascal (1623–62), the French philosopher and
mathematician, struck a fine balance between his intellect and his heart. His intellectual achievements were
substantial, but he didn't neglect the intuitive, emotional dimension of experience. The inner reality of
the heart's knowledge is precious beyond telling, and
Pascal was intimately familiar with it. To be aware of
the heart's reasons, to honor its knowing, is to be true
to yourself in the positive sense. What the heart sees,
intuits, and knows through its affective capacity is
more significant than what we can know through reason. Reason is not in touch with the heart's concerns:
love, compassion, kindness, mercy, faith, union with
the Divine. By attending to them, we become more
human and more divine.

You cannot do a kindness too soon,
for you never know how soon it will be too late.

— Anonymous

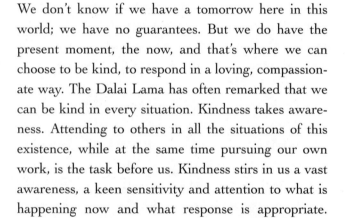

We don't know if we have a tomorrow here in this world; we have no guarantees. But we do have the present moment, the now, and that's where we can choose to be kind, to respond in a loving, compassionate way. The Dalai Lama has often remarked that we can be kind in every situation. Kindness takes awareness. Attending to others in all the situations of this existence, while at the same time pursuing our own work, is the task before us. Kindness stirs in us a vast awareness, a keen sensitivity and attention to what is happening now and what response is appropriate. Never lose an opportunity to do some good today. You never know what tomorrow will bring.

The vision floods the eyes with light, but it is not a light showing some other object; the light is itself the Vision.

— Plotinus

Plotinus (203–70), the Greek mystic philosopher who influenced Western mysticism and philosophical thought with his Neoplatonism, here illumines for us a key to the nature of mystical union with the One. So many mystics in every tradition speak of the Divine as light. Yet few of us consider, as physicist Peter Russell writes, that God literally is this light. Our human eyes cannot take the intensity, brightness, and immensity of this light. We understand that God has no form, but is pure light, the light of infinite consciousness. This light is consciousness in the act of revealing, while consciousness is light in the act of knowing. We are all part of this light, and we reflect its nature in our awareness. If you desire with all your heart integration with the Divine light, you will have it.

Love is difficult, because loving is not enough:
Like God, we must ourselves be Love.

— Angelus Silesius

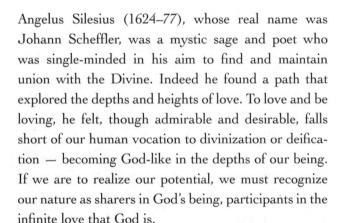

Angelus Silesius (1624–77), whose real name was Johann Scheffler, was a mystic sage and poet who was single-minded in his aim to find and maintain union with the Divine. Indeed he found a path that explored the depths and heights of love. To love and be loving, he felt, though admirable and desirable, falls short of our human vocation to divinization or deification — becoming God-like in the depths of our being. If we are to realize our potential, we must recognize our nature as sharers in God's being, participants in the infinite love that God is.

[137]

Unwrap your gentleness,
for your gentleness is your courage.

— Ma Jaya Sati Bhagavati

⌒

Ma Jaya, or Ma as she is called by her students and friends, is a Jewish-Hindu interfaith spiritual teacher well known for her ministry to those infected with HIV-AIDS. Her life embodies compassionate service. Like the notion of Tibetan teacher Chogyam Trungpa's idea of the spiritual warrior or Dan Millman's notion of the peaceful warrior, Ma Jaya's idea about gentleness strikes a subtle, paradoxical principle of true courage. Although we typically associate courage with bold strength or violent action, an aware gentleness — a gentleness that lets down our defenses and opens us with compassion to the suffering of others — is the true sign of courage. Gentleness can require that we forgo self-defense and embrace vulnerability. But even more, gentleness sees through the falseness of violence, brutality, indifference, and insensitivity. It is the act of courage and persistence in the pursuit of love.

[138]

There are two ways of love —
my selfish way, and Yours above.
My selfish love is when I find
I yearn to grasp you in my mind.
Pure love is when you took the veil from my devoted look.

— Rabi'a al-Adawiya

Rabi'a al-Adawiya (d. 801), the inspired Sufi saint, originated love mysticism in Sufism. The distinction he makes here would escape the attention of most of our cerebral culture. We want to control reality through knowledge. We yearn to know, to grasp, to pin down, to describe precisely. Yet our culture doesn't want to pay the price of such knowledge, which is surrender to the Mystery. Surrender involves letting go of our attempts to comprehend God with our limited intellectual resources; it means approaching the Divine with mystical openness and a vulnerability to the Divine's wishes and actions. Selfish love wants control, whereas pure love mercifully removes the veil that hides God and allows us to see through intimacy with the Divine One. May the Divine remove our selfishness and allow us to know him directly.

[139]

Seek in reading and you will find in meditation.
Knock in prayer and it will be opened to you
in contemplation.

— St. John of the Cross

St. John of the Cross beautifully identifies with great
simplicity the contemplative method of the monastic
tradition called *Lectio Divina.* The entire method is
summed up in this maxim by the Spanish mystic. *Lectio
Divina* in its literal translation means "divine reading"
and really is a form of spiritual practice — reading for
the sake of acquiring inspiration rather than information, reading to prepare ourselves for mystical experience through contemplation. One reads a paragraph, a
page, or a few pages until one feels inspired. Then one
enters the second step, that of meditation or reflection.
Reflection seeks a spark for prayer; when it's found,
the third step into affective prayer begins. This third
step, the prayer of the heart, engages the emotions. At
the end of the third step comes contemplation itself, a
resting in the Divine Presence.

[140]

A raindrop dripping from a cloud
was ashamed when it saw the sea.
"Who am I where there is a sea?" it said.
When it saw itself with the eye of humility,
a shell nurtured it in its embrace.

— Sa'di

⌒

Musharrif al-Din Ben Muslih Sa'di (1215–92), the Persian mystic and poet, presents us with a poetic glimpse of mystical union. This is a classic expression of the mystical union: We seem so tiny compared to the infinite immensity of the Divine. It raises the question for some: Is our identity obliterated in the ultimate union? The vast majority of mystics say no. When we understand this relationship of the raindrop to the sea, the soul in the light of humility, we begin to grasp that we have a place in the Divine Ocean, just as the shell protects the identity and integrity of the raindrop. Do not fear to be that raindrop! Open yourself up to God's welcoming sea and allow yourself a place in his Presence.

Being is and cannot not be.

— Parmenides

⌒

Parmenides (c. 512–445 B.C.E.), a pre-Socratic Greek philosopher, probably came out of the Pythagorean school of mathematical thinkers. This insight about the necessity of being, the impossibility of not being, was an overpowering illumination for him, becoming the basis of his philosophy. His vision of the Divine is that because it exists, non-Being cannot exist. Everything depends on the weight of Being. His illumination laid the foundation in the West for metaphysics, the science of the absolute, which reached a peak in the twentieth century with German philosopher Martin Heidegger. His vision was so absolute that its intense intellectual necessity opens a door to certitude. It is an example of intellect merging with the thrust of the mind/heart toward the Divine Reality.

*Chant the name while sitting, standing, walking, eating,
and in bed and everywhere. The name is omnipotent.*

— Chaitana

Chaitana (c. 1485–1533 B.C.E.) was an Indian saint
from what has come to be known as Krishna Consciousness. This Hindu school emphasizes the person-
alist approach to the Divine, especially a loving
relationship with the avatar Krishna, an incarnation of
Vishnu, one of the absolute forms of the Godhead.
Chaitana reveals to us the importance of remembering
the Divine through chanting the name of God in all the
situations of life. The practice of constant chanting
develops mindfulness of the Presence. For Chaitana,
chanting the name keeps the mind and heart focused
on God at all times. It makes our consciousness subtle
and pure, bringing us into harmony and intimacy with
God. Chanting allows us to reach the Divine's fre-
quency of vibration. In reaching it we know God.

There is no formula to teach us how to arrive at maturity,
and there is no grammar for the language
of the inner life.

— Dag Hammarskjöld

Dag Hammarskjöld, the second Secretary General of the United Nations, was a great peacemaker and a mystic, as his book *Markings* reveals. This quotation is really an autobiographical comment on his own inner development as a mystic in the world, in the secular environment of the United Nations. As a sage in the center of the world body, he often had to make his own way without guidance. His experience demonstrates a fundamental truth of the inner journey: Each person is totally unique without a magical formula to guide him, and everyone is alone on the path. There are norms and advice from our faiths, but each one of us has to arrive at maturity in our own way in harmony with our individual nature and gifts. Although we have a vast mystical literature, we each have a unique need that must be addressed in the unique way we make the inner journey.

Love the Lord, o my soul. . . . A well without water,
a cow without milk, a shrine in darkness —
so are you without him, o my soul.

— Guru Nanak

Guru Nanak (c. 1469–1539), founder of the Sikh tradition, was a great mystic who learned much from the Indian tradition while navigating between the Hindu and Islamic faiths. He drew heavily from both, adding their insights, methods, and disciplines to his own spiritual experience and genius. His beautiful, lyrical cry — so reminiscent of the biblical psalms — enshrines a universal truth: We are nothing without God, and religion is empty if we neglect the Divine. If we do not pursue God, we remain hungry for nourishment and in a state of darkness. Our souls become barren and fruitless, so much do we need God to actualize our capacity for enlightenment. To be a person is to be in relationship with the Absolute, to be in quest of its truth and the liberation it brings. Does Guru Nanak's plea resonate with your heart?

[145]

More than anything else, the future of civilization depends on the way the two most powerful forces of history, science and religion, settle into relationship with each other.

— Alfred North Whitehead

⌒

Philosopher and mathematician Alfred North White-head recognized that the relationship between the two former antagonists was beginning to become more cooperative and understood the promise that relation-ship would hold. Science and religion represent two ways of knowing, both necessary and both serving the greater good. More and more we will witness science and religion complementing each other's understand-ing of reality and the truth. In fact, the world will remain unstable as long as these worldviews are in con-flict with each other. Harmony between humanity's spiritual yearnings, knowledge, and moral understand-ing on the one hand and its scientific impulse to com-prehend and describe the cosmos and the structure of life on the other can lay the foundation for an enduring peace on our tiny planet. You can assist this process of reconciliation in your life by encouraging scientists and clergy to work together in your community to promote mutual understanding.

If we knew how to adore, then nothing could truly disturb
our peace. We would travel through the world
with the tranquility of the great rivers.

— St. Francis of Assisi

The founder of the Franciscan order, the patron saint of animals, was known to be extremely magnanimous in his empathy for the poor and for other creatures of the world. St. Francis knew how to experience adoration; thus he knew how to be in relationship with God. An everlasting peace is one of the fruits of such union with God. This is the peace that only God can give. It is a solidity of inner certitude about the Presence, and nothing can shake that certitude. It is invincible. In each situation we are immersed in his peace because God is our permanence, our coherence, our future. We are united to that reality which does not pass away. When we focus on adoration of the Divine in the intimacy of union, nothing can disturb us, because everything that might is merely an impermanent event, word, or action.

If you have a heart, you can be saved.

— Abba Pambo

⌒

Abba Pambo is a Desert Father of the fourth century, a
Christian hermit monk living in Egypt. The word *abba*
means *father* and signifies his membership in this movement of early Christianity. The desert tradition of early
monasticism emphasized a kind of Christian humanism
in relationships between and among the brethren, extending to everyone they met. They believed that humility of the heart was the most important virtue in the
spiritual life. For Abba Pambo, to have a heart is to be
governed inwardly by the commitment to humility, as
well as to simply *be* humble. If we have humility of
heart, then we can be saved because we are open to
God; we can hear the Divine's guidance. Humility of
heart allows us to know our woundedness, our passions, and our need for spiritual growth. How is your
heart? Is it awake and humble?

The soul that You have given me, O God, is a pure one.
You have created and formed it; breathed it into me,
and within me You sustain it. So long as I have breath,
I will give thanks to You, O Lord my God.

— Jewish liturgy

This passage from the Jewish liturgy reminds us of our
fundamental innocence when we enter this world. The
purity of the soul, of the personal, immortal identity we
each have, is the result of the Divine breath flowing
into us. This breath of the Divine sustains us in all
things. In breathing the soul, the personal identity, into
each one of us, the Divine is also breathing *itself* into us.
God communicates himself to us in each moment and
often does so by *spiration,* the act of breathing. This
Jewish prayer also reminds us that the only appropriate response to this Divine sustenance is gratitude and
thanksgiving.

*When the Spirit of truth comes, he will guide you
into all truth. . . . He will bring glory to me by taking
from what is mine and making it known to you.*

— John 16:13–14

The power of these words lies in their prophetic function, what they promise and foretell. Jesus tells us he is
one with the Father, who is his Father and ours. This
passage in John's Gospel also suggests that the Spirit
can reveal numerous other insights about Christ that
have not been spoken of in the scriptures. There is
another meaning to this text that applies to us: It is the
Spirit who also knows about our identity and our relationship with the Father. We are one with the Divine,
just as Jesus is, and we are called to the same quality
of intimacy with God as the Son of God enjoys. This
scripture is about Jesus, but it is also about each one of us.

Prayer brings a person to a new birth, as it were.
Its power is so great that nothing,
no degree of suffering,
will stand against it.
— *The Way of the Pilgrim*

The Way of the Pilgrim is a treasure on the contemplative form in the tradition of the Orthodox Church. It has inspired tens of thousands of people and will continue to do so. Its roots go back centuries to the monastic life and even further to the seeds of practice in the Desert Tradition. It compels us to marvel and reflect on the nature and efficacy of prayer to transform us. The form of prayer mentioned here is not casual or superficial, but one that breaks open our understanding of our relationship with God. This intensity of prayer springs from Divine grace and our commitment to intimacy with God. When this prayer opens the heart, it constitutes a new birth, a rebirth in the Absolute. *The Way of the Pilgrim* shows a kind of prayer that becomes contemplation and greatly strengthens those graced by its gift.

[151]

As soon as the waves have stopped and
the lake has become quiet, we see its bottom.
So with the mind when it is calm,
we see what our nature is.

— Swami Vivekananda

⌒

Swami Vivekananda, the nineteenth-century Indian sage, beautifully employs a metaphor to explain the process of meditation. The more we surrender to the discipline of meditation, the more we learn who we are, or rather, the more we explore the roots of our identity in the Absolute, in this instance, the Brahman. When our thoughts are stilled — a difficult task whether we are just beginning or years along the path — and our desires are at rest, we become aware of our immortal nature. We are manifestations of the Godhead's infinite creativity. In seeing who we really are, we pass beneath the surface identity of the ego, the superficial social self we were conditioned to hold and present to others. Our true nature calls us to dwell authentically out of this light of being and to make decisions and act from its truth.

When the wise knows that it is through the great
and omnipresent Spirit in us that we are conscious
in waking or in dreaming, then he goes beyond sorrow.

— Katha Upanishad 4

It is a perennial problem of human life to be ignorant of
the deeper nature of our identity. The Katha Upanishad,
a verse narrative that follows the spiritual journey of a
boy to uncover the nature of reality, uncovers the wisdom that we need to achieve immortality, or as the
Upanishad puts it, to "go beyond sorrow." Achieving
this liberated existence frees us from sorrow because we
overcome the cycle of rebirth. According to the Upanishads, we can only go beyond sorrow when we know
Brahman or God. To know God is what the Hindu tradition calls *brahmavidya,* experiential awareness of the
Divine Reality. It is this reality, its vast awareness and
wisdom, that is behind all our acts of knowing, being,
and thinking. God is this Spirit that makes us conscious
in all the situations of life. Seek to know this Spirit, the
Eternal Self present in all your experience and awareness, and know the happiness of the Divine.

[153]

In a time of universal deceit,
telling the truth is a revolutionary act.

— George Orwell

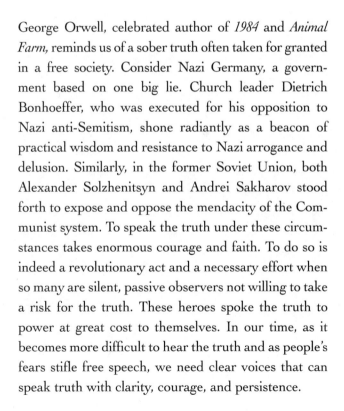

George Orwell, celebrated author of *1984* and *Animal Farm,* reminds us of a sober truth often taken for granted in a free society. Consider Nazi Germany, a government based on one big lie. Church leader Dietrich Bonhoeffer, who was executed for his opposition to Nazi anti-Semitism, shone radiantly as a beacon of practical wisdom and resistance to Nazi arrogance and delusion. Similarly, in the former Soviet Union, both Alexander Solzhenitsyn and Andrei Sakharov stood forth to expose and oppose the mendacity of the Communist system. To speak the truth under these circumstances takes enormous courage and faith. To do so is indeed a revolutionary act and a necessary effort when so many are silent, passive observers not willing to take a risk for the truth. These heroes spoke the truth to power at great cost to themselves. In our time, as it becomes more difficult to hear the truth and as people's fears stifle free speech, we need clear voices that can speak truth with clarity, courage, and persistence.

[154]

When you stand in prayer
and feel that no other joy can be compared to it,
then you have indeed discovered true prayer.

— Evagrius Ponticus

We know the fullness of true prayer when it becomes the priority in our lives. Evagrius Ponticus, the great theologian of mystical prayer, identifies it as great joy. True prayer grants joy from the intimacy with God that one experiences during times of prayer, and it also extends to the rest of one's life. Like meditation, when prayer becomes a true practice, it extends beyond the time we initially devote to it. When prayer becomes the matrix of our lives, enveloping our whole existence, then we are on the right path. Evagrius Ponticus and the other Desert Fathers understood this point very well. They experienced how prayer united them with God and made its practice central to their view of monastic life.

[155]

There's a strange frenzy in my head, of birds flying,
each particle circulating on its own.
Is the one I love everywhere?

— Rumi

Rumi is such a God-intoxicated mystic — a love mystic! He eats, sleeps, lives, dreams, and acts in the Presence. He is totally absorbed in contemplation of the Divine. There is no place he could look or be where he would not find his Beloved, the Divine One. For Rumi, everything that exists reflects God's Presence; everything is charged by the Divine Energy. The Divine surrounds us on all sides and within the depths of the mind, even in the unconscious and on the frontiers of imagination. Such an intimate relationship with God summons total surrender to the Source and a complete commitment to the relationship. Do you wish to be similarly God-intoxicated? Then follow the path outlined by Rumi's life, the single-minded quest for *baqa*, Divine Union with God. Be in love with God beyond reason and concepts, beyond sense and imagination. Allow yourself to be taken into Allah's unity.

[156]

The whole purpose of religion is to facilitate love and compassion, patience, tolerance, humility, and forgiveness.

— The Dalai Lama

While His Holiness's statement might seem like common sense, when we examine the role organized religions sometimes play in our lives, we can see how they can lose their sense of mission. What the Dalai Lama expresses here is the essence of religion and spirituality in the lives of devotees and practitioners. It is not enough to be religious or committed to a religion in practice, nor is it sufficient to be spiritual. Both religion and spirituality must bear fruit in an individual's moral life. I would even question the use of the word *tolerance,* with its connotation of minimal acceptance, a begrudging, passive, live-and-let-live approach. The person transformed through the practice of faith enthusiastically embraces others and their right to pursue their own religion or spiritual path. If a religion does not fuel our growth in these necessary virtues, then it doesn't have much value. And in the end, if we are not transformed through our tradition, we should reappraise our commitment.

[157]

Giving of ourselves to help others works in two ways:
it benefits the recipient and it benefits the giver.

— Robert Lawrence Smith

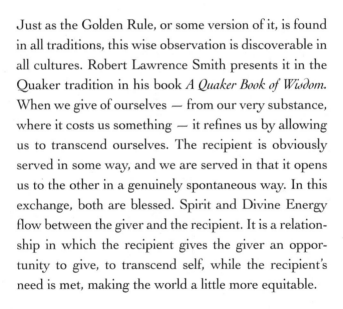

Just as the Golden Rule, or some version of it, is found in all traditions, this wise observation is discoverable in all cultures. Robert Lawrence Smith presents it in the Quaker tradition in his book *A Quaker Book of Wisdom.* When we give of ourselves — from our very substance, where it costs us something — it refines us by allowing us to transcend ourselves. The recipient is obviously served in some way, and we are served in that it opens us to the other in a genuinely spontaneous way. In this exchange, both are blessed. Spirit and Divine Energy flow between the giver and the recipient. It is a relationship in which the recipient gives the giver an opportunity to give, to transcend self, while the recipient's need is met, making the world a little more equitable.

Our universe is but one atom
in a much larger cosmic archipelago.

— Sir Martin Rees

Sir Martin Rees, the Astronomer Royal of Great Britain and research professor at Cambridge University, is the foremost authority on the multiverse, the unlimited amount of other universes in which we are but a speck. If this makes us all feel very, very small, we should take heart in our capacity to grasp this thought. Although quantitatively we are infinitesimally small, qualitatively we are quite large. We are, after all, beings who can discover the unlimited nature of the cosmos and metacosmos. The process of cosmic reflection, mystical contemplation, locates us in a much larger reality. What science calls the universe or universes is not the whole story. Are you open to the other realms to which the experiences of all the mystics point? If not, ask for the grace of openness.

*We can choose to use our lives for others to bring
about a better and more just world for our children.*

— César Chavez

The great Mexican-American activist César Chavez, cofounder of the United Farm Workers, sums up what the real choice is in this life: to serve the needs of the larger good with a constant thought for generations to come rather than the immediate gain of the few we consider our friends. What he is proposing is the spirit of the Gospel and of all the world's great religions, especially the indigenous traditions that remained focused on the larger good of the community. Chavez's vision of social justice and nonviolence mirrored that found in Native American traditions — particularly those that examined how their actions today would affect the next seven generations — as well as the best of Christianity's social justice teachings, the prophetic teachings of the Jewish faith, the emphasis on compassion in Buddhism, the selfless action in Hinduism, and the commitment to justice in the Islamic community. A mature, viable spiritual life requires us to embrace the larger reality of the community and the needs of future generations. Can we say that we live our lives with those needs in mind?

*Compassion is not a sentiment but is making justice
and doing works of mercy. Compassion is not
a moral commandment but a flow and overflow
of the fullest human and divine energies.*

— Matthew Fox

Former Dominican priest Matthew Fox is the founder
of Creation Spirituality, which "integrates the wisdom of
Western spirituality and global indigenous cultures with
the emerging post-modern scientific understanding of the
universe and the awakening artistic passion for creativity which reveals the interrelatedness of all life." His
book *A Spirituality Named Compassion* identifies the practical virtue of compassion: sacred action in the world
that affects individuals, communities, and the natural
world. If we are in meaningful relationship with the
Divine, not simply fulfilling a perfunctory religious obli-
gation — if religion is more to us than a superficial social
function — then we realize that compassion has to be
implemented. It has to affect the suffering of others.
More still, this compassionate action is inspired by the
deepest spiritual forces in us, the intermingling of
the Divine and human capacities of love-in-action.

Teachers open the door. You enter yourself.

— Chinese proverb

⁓

As a teacher, I am very much aware of the truth and wisdom of this adage. It is driven home to me every time I give a lecture. I lead my students, pointing the way, trying to stretch them beyond their current assumptions and awareness. Whether or not their vision of reality is enlarged, it's up to them to change their lives. They have to walk through the door of realization. This Chinese saying also emphasizes the reality of free will and the lonely nature of the individual path. Mythologist Joseph Campbell revealed the necessity of the individual journey by relating his favorite story in Arthurian legend: When the knights of the Round Table embarked on their search for the Holy Grail, they did so individually, each knight entering the forest at the darkest point, where there was no path for him to follow. "Where there's a way or path, it is someone else's path," Campbell wrote. "Each human being is a unique phenomenon."

[162]

*A person's true wealth
is the good he does in this world.*

— Muhammad

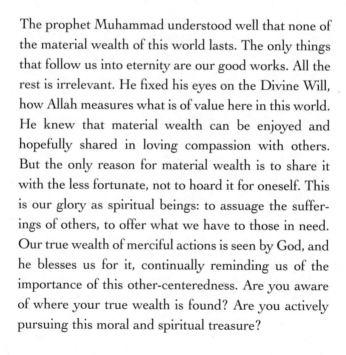

The prophet Muhammad understood well that none of
the material wealth of this world lasts. The only things
that follow us into eternity are our good works. All the
rest is irrelevant. He fixed his eyes on the Divine Will,
how Allah measures what is of value here in this world.
He knew that material wealth can be enjoyed and
hopefully shared in loving compassion with others.
But the only reason for material wealth is to share it
with the less fortunate, not to hoard it for oneself. This
is our glory as spiritual beings: to assuage the sufferings of others, to offer what we have to those in need.
Our true wealth of merciful actions is seen by God, and
he blesses us for it, continually reminding us of the
importance of this other-centeredness. Are you aware
of where your true wealth is found? Are you actively
pursuing this moral and spiritual treasure?

[163]

*Curiosity is one of the permanent
and certain characteristics
of a vigorous intellect.*

— Samuel Johnson

A vigorous intellect is never satisfied with easy and conventional answers, but looks deeper below the surface. Writer Samuel Johnson was of course such a vigorous mind, wedded to an incredible wit. This mental attribute of curiosity is the basis of all great science, philosophy, art, poetry, literature, and music. It is a twin to that other indispensable quality: imagination. Some people go through life with little curiosity about what really matters: how to lead spiritually and humanly fulfilling and significant lives. They may get bogged down into a kind of petty curiosity about others, the kind of curiosity fueled by gossip, but not the true passionate curiosity that drives human creativity. Identifying our passions and following them, no matter what others say, can inspire our curiosity. This is a central task of life.

[164]

Science is concerned with the workings of the cosmos, while religion is concerned with the meaning behind it.

— Brother David Steindl-Rast

Brother David Steindl-Rast, a Benedictine monk who has deeply influenced interspiritual dialogue, has hold of a very basic distinction that makes clear an important truth often obscured by scientists and philosophers. I've heard it said that science is concerned with describing the universe, not explaining it, and if we look closely we realize this is true. As science progresses, it paints more detailed and sophisticated views of the large and the small, making the connections to describe how things work. But is it really *explaining* anything about our universe? Is it identifying the deeper meaning behind the genome it is mapping? This is where religion's value comes in and where science and religion can build deeper and more satisfying means of supporting each other. Meaning often eludes the scientific enterprise, and sometimes in their enthusiasm over the practical benefits of technological achievements, scientists will conflate fact with meaning, thinking themselves masters of meaning because of their extraordinary grasp of the facts. Facts change in science, and so does our interpretation of facts. Meanings evolve in our understanding. Respect the facts but always seek the deeper meaning.

[165]

*The end and aim of all education
is the development of character.*
— Francis W. Parker

⌒

Education has to go to the roots of the personality and effect change, transforming attitudes, dispositions, and the fundamental commitment of the individual. The Greeks, from which so much of the Western tradition is derived, placed great emphasis on the development of character, and this goal was the chief rationale for sports and Olympic competition. The medieval Christian ideal of learning also focused on the education of the whole person: body, soul, and spirit. In the East, the Tibetan tradition places great emphasis on the good heart, and this good heart is the aim of much Buddhist practice and education. My uncle, John Cosgrove, himself a college professor, used to say, "Our universities are filled with people who have brilliant minds but stupid hearts!" We simply pay too much attention to facts and skills and not enough to fostering responsibility, ethics, charity, and kindness.

[166]

*You cannot enter the door of yoga
without kindness and compassion for others.*

— Changkya

Changkya (1717–86) was a Tibetan Buddhist master of
yoga who taught the seventh Dalai Lama and the
Emperor of China. The ancient Yogic tradition went far
beyond the physical postures and practices of Hatha
Yoga that we have embraced in the West. It is an entire
tradition designed around the path to enlightenment.
The essence of yoga is transformation of the heart. As
a practice, it is ultimately about union with Ultimate
Reality or the unconditioned state of being that is fully
awake and aware, awake to the nature of the truth
and aware of our deeper, eternal nature. Yoga recon-
nects us with the Source and frees us from the lesser
impulses of the ego, the instinctual desires, and the false
self. Yoga has to be grounded in compassion and kindness. In order to practice yoga effectively, we have to
bring an awakened heart and mind to the activity.

[167]

To love always and love all. To be able to say at the
end of each day: "I loved in every moment."
— Chiara Lubich

⁓

To be able to say at the end of a day that you "loved in
every moment" is obviously an extraordinary accomplishment. Even if one can manage to love in every
moment of the day, the real accomplishment is to love
everyone without discriminating between those you
like and those you don't. Chiara Lubich, founder of the
Focolare Movement, a lay Catholic organization of five
million people committed to prayer, social action, and
following the Gospel's exhortation to put love into
action, is an apostle of Divine Love in our time. The
Focolare Movement is present in a hundred and
eighty-seven countries, focusing daily on living the
Gospel concretely in the world, especially through its
interfaith work. Wherever members of this vigorous
community live, they are known for their selfless love
in their attitudes and actions. By simply communicating this living essence of the Gospel, Chiara Lubich
embodies this extraordinary focus on Divine Love.

The body trembles, the tongue falters, the mind is weary.
Forsaking them all, I pursue my purpose happily.

— Ashtavakra Gita

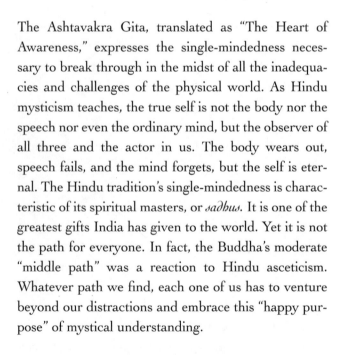

The Ashtavakra Gita, translated as "The Heart of Awareness," expresses the single-mindedness necessary to break through in the midst of all the inadequacies and challenges of the physical world. As Hindu mysticism teaches, the true self is not the body nor the speech nor even the ordinary mind, but the observer of all three and the actor in us. The body wears out, speech fails, and the mind forgets, but the self is eternal. The Hindu tradition's single-mindedness is characteristic of its spiritual masters, or *sadhus*. It is one of the greatest gifts India has given to the world. Yet it is not the path for everyone. In fact, the Buddha's moderate "middle path" was a reaction to Hindu asceticism. Whatever path we find, each one of us has to venture beyond our distractions and embrace this "happy purpose" of mystical understanding.

[169]

A victory of spirit always comes before
any material victory.

— Bojana Kovacevic

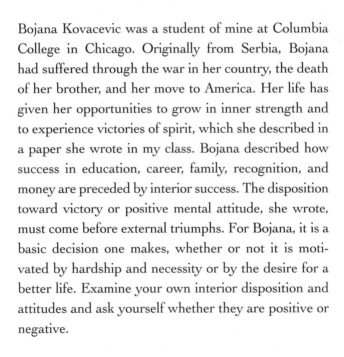

Bojana Kovacevic was a student of mine at Columbia College in Chicago. Originally from Serbia, Bojana had suffered through the war in her country, the death of her brother, and her move to America. Her life has given her opportunities to grow in inner strength and to experience victories of spirit, which she described in a paper she wrote in my class. Bojana described how success in education, career, family, recognition, and money are preceded by interior success. The disposition toward victory or positive mental attitude, she wrote, must come before external triumphs. For Bojana, it is a basic decision one makes, whether or not it is motivated by hardship and necessity or by the desire for a better life. Examine your own interior disposition and attitudes and ask yourself whether they are positive or negative.

Patience is bitter but its fruit is sweet.

— Jean Jacques Rousseau

No one likes to wait; we are all in a rush to get somewhere, achieve results, be a success, maybe even to attain enlightenment. Jean Jacques Rousseau (1712–78), the great Swiss Romantic philosopher and political theorist, highlights how it usually takes a lot of waiting to achieve anything. In fact, the French have a saying: "With a little patience we arrive at everything." Early in life we learn the bitter truth that we have to wait: for Christmas, for a visit from a friend or family member, to reach our destination on a family vacation. Later in life we wait for that needed vacation, a new car, for wisdom, for the dawn to come. Maybe what we want will never come. Zen Buddhists are fond of reminding us that we may sit our entire lives and never experience *kensho* (enlightenment). So we must realize that the point of sitting is just that: sitting.

[171]

Life is ... a sand tray,
if we let the unconscious come through.
Revelation is right there.

— Marion Weber

⌒

Marion Weber, founder of the Arts and Healing Network, identifies here a vehicle of creativity, illumination, and insight. The unconscious is unbound by time, space, and the laws of physics. It exists completely open to all that is, has been, or will be in the eternal now. If we can position ourselves through intention and practice, attitude and availability to this vehicle of more ultimate knowing, then we have access to revelation. I have always thought that revelation is an ongoing process; it exists at all times and in all places, in every dimension of reality and experience. One of the usual channels for the unconscious is the dream state, in which we are open and more at ease, where conscious control has given way. Relaxation, meditation, walking, listening to music, yoga, and contemplating art are all ways to dispose ourselves to the call of the unconscious, the influence of revelation or mystical insight. It is always there surrounding us on every side.

Deep feelings are the voices that need to be heard and expressed to find our transformation.

— Anne Brener

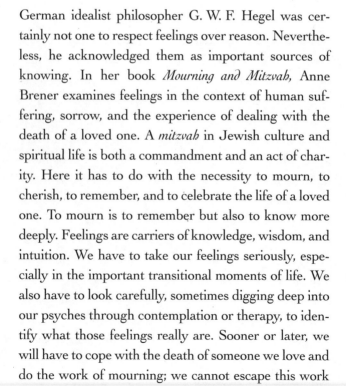

German idealist philosopher G. W. F. Hegel was certainly not one to respect feelings over reason. Nevertheless, he acknowledged them as important sources of knowing. In her book *Mourning and Mitzvah,* Anne Brener examines feelings in the context of human suffering, sorrow, and the experience of dealing with the death of a loved one. A *mitzvah* in Jewish culture and spiritual life is both a commandment and an act of charity. Here it has to do with the necessity to mourn, to cherish, to remember, and to celebrate the life of a loved one. To mourn is to remember but also to know more deeply. Feelings are carriers of knowledge, wisdom, and intuition. We have to take our feelings seriously, especially in the important transitional moments of life. We also have to look carefully, sometimes digging deep into our psyches through contemplation or therapy, to identify what those feelings really are. Sooner or later, we will have to cope with the death of someone we love and do the work of mourning; we cannot escape this work and opportunity. Grieving has a gift in it.

We are a single community, the planet Earth,
and we live or die together. There's no such thing
as human advantage. The universe is a communion
of subjects, not a collection of objects. Our relationship with
the natural world is not primarily stewardship.
It's primarily rapport, admiration,
interaction with, and listening to.

— Thomas Berry

One of the foremost ecological thinkers in our time, nature mystic Thomas Berry is a geologian, a theologian for the Earth. He argues that we consistently view ourselves as separate from the Earth and our fellow inhabitants. Our actual role is one of intrinsic interdependence, with a potential for communion with other subjects across species and with the Earth itself. We don't have much choice if we want to survive. We have to awaken to this larger perspective, this wisdom of the Earth. There can be no passive observers since we all have a responsibility for our planet. Rather than dominating and subjugating the natural world, we are here to develop a deeper relationship of intimacy with nature, one that is characterized by a deeper listening, harmony, interaction, and affinity. This relationship is a way into the Divine Mystery.

Know yourself: a cloud drifting before your sun.
Cut yourself off from your senses
and behold your sun of intimacy.

— Fakhruddin 'Iraqi

Fakhruddin 'Iraqi (1213–89), Persian mystic and poet, here explores the Sufi notions of *fana* and *baqa*. Fana is annihilation of the self, the letting go of ourselves into the Divine, while *baqa* is about union with Allah or God. Like many Christian mystics, Fakhruddin expresses the relationship in the language of love mysticism. This wise Sufi tells us to cut ourselves off from our senses to attain union. The senses and reason are usually concerned with external matters, but this mystic stresses the necessity of abandoning them in the pursuit of the Divine and intimacy with it. Like a "cloud before the sun," we are immersed in our senses, but once we abandon them before God, we find intimacy with God.

[175]

The dream of the ashram is perhaps one of the greatest
gifts which India can give to humanity as a whole.

— Jyoti Sahi

The ashram is a community, often led by a teacher
or guru, organized around prayer, meditation, yoga, or
spiritual teaching. Jyoti Sahi, one of India's greatest
artists, believed this unique Hindu institution could
remind humanity of the power of small communities.
Similar in some ways to a monastery in the Christian
tradition, though open to both men and women, or
similar even to Israel's secular *kibbutzim*, the ashram is
usually dedicated to mystical life. Anyone may come to
an ashram and stay for a few days, weeks, or even
months. My spiritual teacher Father Bede Griffiths
believed that small communities would be the salvation
of humanity. He placed his faith in Shantivanum, his
Hindu-Christian ashram on the banks of the sacred
Kavery River in south India. I believe the ashram can
help more developed countries, which are often overwhelmed by the demands of modernity, find resonance
with their deepest aspirations to live more spiritually.

The soul is the sense of something higher
than ourselves, something that stirs in us thoughts,
hopes, and aspirations which go out to the world
of goodness, truth, and beauty.

— Albert Schweitzer

Albert Schweitzer acknowledged that we don't really have any specific way to define the soul, but we can nonetheless know what it is. The most religious among us and the least religious among us might agree with Schweitzer's idea of the soul. It requires a belief in goodness, truth, and beauty more than a belief in God, but it fits with a mystic's notion of God as well. May we be stirred by his idea of the soul and recognize it in ourselves.

[177]

When we get to heaven we shall find that everything is held for the good of all in common.

— Mechthild of Magdeburg

In the early ages of the Church, Christians were distinguished by the way they loved one another and served the needs of each other in the community. We are part of a much greater reality than ourselves, our families, and our circles of friends. One of the goals of life is to learn the value of community, of interconnectedness, our oneness in the Divine Reality. Social enlightenment is the keen realization of this truth and the commitment to live it in day-to-day experience. Our notions of private property and ownership are human contrivances that God and nature do not recognize. As we strive for the heavenly ideal, we should work together to set forth a path for humanity that includes everybody. That's the Divine Will for the human family, and the best in each religion acknowledges a similar vision. Let us become open to genuine community, to extending ourselves beyond our loved ones.

[178]

*It is not for him to pride himself who loves his own country,
but rather for him who loves the whole world.
The earth is but one country and mankind its citizens.*

— Baha'u'llah

Baha'u'llah, the founder of the Baha'i tradition in Iran,
saw the terrible toll the nation state and blind nationalism took and would continue to take in world history.
Love of one's own country, although admirable, could
not hold as a virtue for the whole world. Our own age,
a hundred and fifty years after Baha'u'llah's, is proving
his adage again, with the inevitable forces of globalism
bringing the human family together — for good and
bad. The retrogressive forces of tribalism and narrow
notions of culture and religion are reacting violently to
this inevitable trend, but the coming together of the
planet as one community cannot be stopped. The planet
itself is our real nation, and we are all members of that
larger society. The enlightened have to put the interests
of humankind and the natural world before the interests of individual communities. This is the demand of
our time.

[179]

When you act as an angel, you are kind, compassionate,
helpful, and true to your word.

— Yogi Bhajan

⌒

The Sikh spiritual leader Yogi Bhajan expresses in a
lyrical way a very basic truth about the holiness of life.
We are not angels, nor are we "earning our wings," but
we are capable in our true nature of being angelic or
God-like. When we are like angels in our capacity to
care, to love, to be kind, and to be always available for
others, we are becoming a new humanity. In the Christian tradition we are said to be in the image and likeness
of God; in the Buddhist faith we have the Buddha-
nature. Allow your divine, angelic, Buddha-nature to
express itself in your life, being, attitudes, and actions.
Be the angel you ultimately are!

[180]

Every language is a petrified philosophy.

— Max Muller

Max Muller (1823–1900), a talented philologist and ori-
entalist, translator, and general editor of *The Sacred Books
of the East* series, understood that each language is a
repository of a people's history, culture, mentality, philosophical insight, moral values, and spiritual experience.
All that a people has acquired through the centuries is
housed in their language. The written word and its spoken expression is also an orientation to life. One can
even say it is metaphysical, a hidden view of the nature
of existence, the natural world, and the cosmos. Sometimes that petrified philosophy can be retrogressive and
block the possibility of real progress. It is necessary for
each one of us to examine our use of language from time
to time to become clear about the philosophy we assume
in it. How does this relate to the mystical life? A hidden
metaphysics or philosophy, if it is not wise, can hold us
back from where we need to go. Regard your own use
of language and discern the philosophical assumptions
you are making, even unconsciously. Ask yourself if
these assumptions serve the well-being of the Earth and
all beings and if they enhance your spiritual life.

The act of painting is a spiritual covenant
between the maker and the higher powers.
— Audrey Flack

⌒

Audrey Flack, a brilliant artist, shares her creative
process in her book *Art and Soul: Notes on Creating,* argu-
ing that every work is a collaboration between the person and the Divine. It is also a "covenant," as she
observes, an agreement that one's art, whatever form it
may take, is a cooperative venture in which the artist is
both a vehicle and an agent of self-expression. The creative person always has sufficient room to render their
inspiration concretely in the chosen medium. The artist
always has a uniqueness that comes through, a singular artistic vision, yet as so many artists acknowledge,
they are also a conduit for a larger creative spirit. Each
one of us has our own creativity, our own special talent, and this should also be open to collaboration with
the Divine and the inspiration it provides.

A miracle is not an unusual event but an event to which we pay unusual attention.

— Ron Miller

Our existence in this world is surrounded by miracles, but we hardly notice. Ron Miller, writer and professor of religious studies at Lake Forest College, says that these events become miraculous for us simply when we pay attention. If we want to experience the miraculous, we have to allow ourselves to notice. I believe the greatest miracles in life are miracles of grace, those moments when there is a deep change of heart. People who have been estranged for years begin to reconcile with each other, a drug addict wakes up and abandons his addiction, an alienated son or daughter returns home to his or her parents. Are you aware of the miracles in your life?

Through stillness joined to insight true,
his passions are annihilated. Stillness
must first of all be found. That springs
from disregarding worldly satisfactions.

— Buddhist scripture

This statement from a compilation of Buddhist scriptures edited by Edward Conze takes us into the living heart of meditation. The work of the meditative process is silencing the mind, bringing it to stillness. Stillness of mind and desire happen when there is a detachment from the cravings of the body. One doesn't need to reject the cravings but to regard them from a different perspective that understands the necessity of being free of their control. If we don't, we remain in a state of psychological bondage. No progress in the spiritual journey is possible without inner freedom from the compulsion of desire. But this only happens when we have the will and determination to become free and are guided by genuine insight into the necessity of freedom. If these conditions are present, passions release their hold.

If people think of God as much as they think
of the world, who would not attain liberation?

— Maitri Upanishad

The spiritual journey begins with getting our priorities in order. A good friend of mine is a "sportsaholic." His entire life revolves around baseball. He even spends every off-season researching players' records and team statistics. "You know, Jim," I told him one day, "if you spent as much time on your spiritual life as you spend on baseball, you'd be a saint!" Even in ancient India, the source of the Maitri, worldly distractions kept people from spiritual matters. If we are to achieve liberation today, amidst extraordinary distractions, we have to pay more attention to God, which translates practically into putting more time each day into our spiritual life. There is no substitute for the hard work of dedicated spiritual discipline. Liberation doesn't happen in a vacuum; it requires an ongoing commitment that becomes more urgent with time.

I have decided that I do not want to kill. I see a sheep in the field — let it live; I see a cow in the field — let it live; I see some other creature — let it live. I do not want to kill for me.

— John B. S. Coats

John Coats, a dedicated animal rights activist and ecologist, calls our attention to the fundamental choice we have to make about recognizing the rights of other species. It starts with each one of us; we have to take the issue into our everyday decisions, how we conduct our daily existence. The reason why so many people can so easily eat animals is because they don't really see the sentient beings they are consuming; we have been completely removed from actually killing the animals we eat. We do not see the conditions they live in or the lives they lead. It's better for the appetite not to look! When we see a cow, a sheep, a chicken, or some other bird and connect with it, we are stirred perhaps to let it be. Or maybe we will continue to consume animals but with a conscious respect for the creatures that give us sustenance. A sense of responsibility is awakened when we encounter animals as fellow creatures. Our diet is an ethical decision we each make for ourselves, but we should at the very least think about the decision.

The contemplation of Eternity makes the Soul immortal.

— Thomas Traherne

The poet and writer Thomas Traherne understood that immortality has to be worked at; we have to develop our connection to immortality as we would build muscles. Jewish philosopher Moses Maimonides and countless others from various traditions have realized that immortality isn't assured but requires a spiritual life to be attained. Immortality, the poet reminds us, comes about as the soul enters contemplation of eternity, for like unites with like, the immortal soul with the Eternal One. The act of mystical contemplation increases the capacities of the soul and gives the soul vital exercise in the higher ways of knowing, being, and acting. Contemplation of eternity makes the soul like the eternal, and this results in an activated capacity for the eternal, which becomes immortality. To meditate on eternity involves all that eternity is, and this leads to the consideration of the cosmic mysteries and the substantial truth that the Divine is love itself. Contemplation of eternity, therefore, is also an immersion into Divine Love. It is a mystical union.

The only true wisdom lives far from mankind, out in the great loneliness, and it can be reached only through suffering. Privation and suffering alone can open the mind of a person to all that is hidden to others.

— Igjugarjuk

Innumerable indigenous cultures are nourished by contact with the Divine Presence in the natural world. Igjugarjuk, an early-twentieth-century Caribou Eskimo shaman, shares a deeply understood truth of native peoples everywhere. It is epitomized in the vision quest of the Native Americans. It reflects the universal insight that definitive contact with God occurs when we withdraw from the world to gather perspective and make space for the Divine to reveal itself to us. In the wilderness, untouched by humanity, free and open to the influence of the maintaining Source, we are in a position to receive an untainted wisdom. But to withdraw to these vast spaces, the first world, is to pay the price of the wisdom it gives. Like the vision quest and its demands, such wisdom extracts a cost from us. We have to change in some essential way. We have to deny ourselves so the Divine can reveal itself to us. Are you ready to look in the direction of native peoples? If so, be prepared to change.

*My dancing, my drinking, and singing weave me
the mat on which my soul will sleep in the world of spirits.*

— Old Man of Halmahera

This lyrical exaltation of the place of imagination in the spiritual journey suggests that our experiences in this life become memories on which we may draw in the "world of spirits." In that realm of spirits, our memories, joys, laughter — indeed, every significant experience in this life — are dream contents for the next life. Our ecstatic experiences are a bridge to the other world, and they accompany us into death and sleep, but this is not a sleep of death, of nothingness or oblivion, but a play of the imagination in the dream consciousness. In the world of spirits, our memories are vivid and powerful icons of experience that give us focus. How will your memories serve you? Are they filled with joyful moments? Seek to develop these memories, for they become vehicles of your dreams beyond this world.

God is an infinite sphere whose center is everywhere
and whose circumference is nowhere.

— Meister Eckhart

⌒

This aphorism is from a twelfth-century Latin hermetic work called *The Book of the Twenty-four Philosophers,* and it has appeared in many versions ever since it first surfaced. St. Bonaventure, the Franciscan of the thirteenth century, incorporates it in his mystical writing *Intinerarium mentis in Deum,* or *The Soul's Journey into God.* This metaphor for the Absolute has proven to be effective and powerful in communicating the mystery of the Source. Every place is the center because God is an infinite, intelligible sphere — totally unlimited and undetermined. Wherever the Divine is, that is the center. In some versions of this metaphor, the word *intelligible* is employed instead of the word *infinite.* This means that something of God can be understood, but just as the circumference is ungraspable, much of the Divine is beyond our comprehension. Take this profound analogy and sit with it for a few years!

When I would recreate myself, I seek the darkest wood,
the thickest and most interminable, and to the citizen,
most dismal swamp. I enter the swamp
as a sacred place — a sanctum sanctorum.
There is the strength, the marrow of Nature.

— Henry David Thoreau

Henry David Thoreau's method of being in communion with the natural world was simply to walk, a practice he celebrated in his work *Walking*. Thoreau's cathedral was the vast wilderness, where he discovered the unmitigated wildness of the Divine itself. Here he tells us that to restore himself he enters the thick, dark woods and finds a lonely swamp. He knows that the swamp is a sacred place, "a *sanctum sanctorum*," or a holy of holies. Its darkness didn't scare Thoreau. He understood the truth these remote places held: that nature is perhaps the most enduring, most significant source of vision and strength for us all. The darkness we humans fear in nature is precisely what we must confront and examine to reveal its own unknowable truth.

[191]

Call the world if you please, "The Vale of Soul Making."
Then you will find out the use of the world.

— John Keats

John Keats, the English Romantic poet, like Thoreau, made a religion of nature. The world of the human community, and the world of nature surrounding it, nurtures, sustains, and inspires us aesthetically and spiritually. The world in both senses is a place of formation and education for the soul. The world around us is our teacher, the environment of our growth into mature human and spiritual beings. In this education, the worlds of humanity and wildness converge. It is precisely through our human development in its spiritual and moral capacities that we come into our own as persons. The world in both senses, and ones we haven't even considered, is a school where we are learning how to love more fully. We are all in the process of soul making.

God is to the soul what the sun is to the earth.

— Hildegard of Bingen

⌒

Many sages, philosophers, and mystics have used this analogy in trying to describe the relationship with the Divine Reality. In *The Republic,* for example, in his dialogue on the perfect system of government and the nature of true justice, Plato employs the metaphor of the sun to represent God, or the Good, as he calls the Absolute. Hildegard of course is speaking in a more personal, mystical context. As the soul's sun, God provides everything we need to sustain and encourage our growth — materially, psychologically, aesthetically, spiritually, and morally. At the same time, the Divine sun communicates itself through grace to the soul in a hidden or mystical way. There is an entire order of grace at work in the spiritual life that goes on beyond the perception of others. As the sun provides so much for the Earth, God is the source of everything for the soul.

I enjoy the silence in a church before the service
more than any sermon.

— Ralph Waldo Emerson

Emerson's quip wasn't meant to be disrespectful; it is the true sentiment of a contemplative spirit drawn to the revelations and rejuvenating power of stillness, the silence where the Divine Presence dwells. Emerson, the great transcendental mystic, is like the countless ranks of the unchurched who have left traditional spiritual communities but who maintain a longing for genuine spirituality. Many of these people have experienced substantial tastes of mystical spirituality but find it difficult to attend a church, synagogue, mosque, or temple because these institutions fail to give their flocks the spiritual sustenance they need. Attracted to the peace and illumination of silence, we can experience the calm joy that results from contact with Divine silence. Thomas Keating calls silence "God's language." Emerson was conversant with this language, just as we all may be.

*Beauty takes us beyond the visible to the height
of consciousness, past the ordinary to the mystical,
away from the expedient to the endlessly true.*

— Joan Chittister

As Sister Joan Chittister, a Benedictine nun, spiritual writer, and activist, remarks in her compelling gem *Illuminated Life: Monastic Wisdom for Seekers of Light*, beauty is our gateway to the mystical, as absolute in life as in eternity. As the Greeks discovered and the poets remembered, beauty is an attribute of God. The encounter with beauty carries us beyond this world to the summit of consciousness, takes us through the ordinary to the transcendent, breaking through the temporal to what is absolutely and eternally true. All beauty is the call of the Divine. Allow yourself to luxuriate in the presence of beauty whenever you have the opportunity. It is an ambassador of the Ultimate.

Dew evaporates and all our world is dew…
so dear, so refreshing, so fleeting.

— Issa

⌒

The Japanese Zen Buddhist Issa (1763–1827) wrote these koan-like words after the death of his beloved child. They express the fundamental Buddhist metaphysical principle of impermanence, *sunyata,* or emptiness. Despite the terrible ache we all feel as those we love pass away, we can take comfort in the beauty and inevitability of the cycle, as Issa touched on with his poetry: that rebirth comes from death. Our lives are bounded by impermanence. It measures our days in this passing world. Jean Houston once said to me: "When we look at the extent of cosmic time, our lives are as brief as fleas." The brevity of life should alert us to the purpose of our existence: to grow in compassion, kindness, love, and sensitivity. Time is short and there is so much to learn, to be, and to do. Impermanence frames the field of our growth. Focus on what is necessary and leave all else behind.

Very often, the inertia and repugnance
which characterize the so-called 'spiritual life'
of many Christians could perhaps be cured
by a simple respect for the concrete realities
of every-day life, for nature, for the body,
for one's work, one's friends, one's surroundings. . . .
Meditation has no point and no reality
unless it is firmly rooted in life.

— Thomas Merton

Spirituality isn't about the supernatural or denial of the world around us. As Catholic monk Thomas Merton found when he integrated his own Christian faith with the philosophies of the East, spiritual practice should find its sustenance and inspiration in our everyday lives and in the physical world around us.

Yet not in torpor would I find,
Awe is the finest portion of mankind.
However scarce the world may make this sense —
in awe one feels profoundly the immense.

— Goethe

It takes a certain humility and spontaneity to experience the emotion and perception of awe. Johann Wolfgang von Goethe (1749–1832), the German poet, understood that awe characterizes our deepest nature. It is the best part of human nature because it is so grounded in humility and innocence of heart, as well as a worldview that looks beyond the self and its preoccupations. One cannot be mentally lazy and know this awe. It demands and extracts from us an alertness of intellect and being, heart and spirit. Our intuition operates in the experience of awe. It is the working of a higher faculty of knowing. Children are unjaded experts and practitioners of this depth of wonder. Look back and remember the feeling of wonder you felt as a child; work to reactivate your ability to know in this way.

Our discontent is actually a gift of spirit.
It is the backside of the dream, the part of us
that is held back at this moment....
Honoring the discontent is the doorway
into the next dimension of life.

— Mary Manin Morrissey

Mary Manin Morrissey is a minister of the Living Enrich-
ment Center, a church in Oregon, and the author of
Building Your Field of Dreams. She suggests the positive
side of frustration and discontent is the beginning of
discovering your dream. It is a sign that the deeper
aspects of who you are need to find a vehicle to actualization in your life. Whether the frustration you feel is
related to a talent you have that lacks an outlet, a vision
you have of where you want to be, or some creative
project you can't quite get started on, you have to listen to your discontent because it is, as Mary tells us, "a
gift" we give ourselves or the Divine gives us to move
us forward in realizing our dream. We should listen to
the voice of our discontent when it arises and allow it
to clarify our dreams for us. It is an important first step
in the process of reaching our destination.

[199]

No one knows enough to be a pessimist.

— Wayne Dyer

⌒

Wayne Dyer truly understands the nature of genuine spirituality. A person of wisdom has to be a consummate optimist. Pessimism and cynicism are psychological distortions, not perceptions of the real. As Dyer suggests, no human being has seen, has experienced enough, or knows enough to embrace pessimism as a mind-set. The world is full of mysteries and possibilities.

[200]

If you want creativity, then give up predictability.
If you want innovation, then you've got to be
willing to be surprised.

— Margaret Wheatley

Our survival instincts often crave the predictable and the static. Margaret Wheatley, author of *Leadership and the New Science,* presents us with two basic rules to assist our creative process: spontaneity and receptivity to surprise. Creativity is often a nonlinear path, and so predictability can be an obstacle to its free-flowing development. It can obstruct the imagination by re-routing it into routine. But it's not enough to be open to the imagination and free of predictability; we must also embrace surprise. Spontaneity and surprise are close associates of the imagination, and they are the assistants of the great works that emanate from the creative spirit. Have you befriended spontaneity and the capacity for surprise?

[201]

Why become a Buddhist
when you can become a Buddha?

— Lama Surya Das

Tibetan Buddhist Lama Surya Das became well known
with the publication of his great work *Awakening the
Buddha Within*. As Surya Das teaches, Buddhism is
more than choosing a spiritual path; he calls our attention to our deeper nature, the timeless reality of our
ultimate identity as awakened ones, whether we realize
it or not. The "Buddha within" is our own actual
nature, which has become obscured in the course of
our life in this world. Our ignorance of our real nature
obscures the capacities we all have. That is in fact
the purpose of Buddhism: to discover and activate the
Buddha within, our own intrinsic nature shared with
all sentient beings. Have you awakened to who you
really are?

Hang around with people who make you laugh.
Find out what makes you laugh —
and start getting more of that in your life.

— Allen Klein

Laughter is so good for us physically and psychologically. Allen Klein, author of *The Healing Power of Humor,* clearly knows its value. Humor bonds us with others; it builds intimacy, trust, and a positive attitude. Of course humor sometimes holds deeper truths, and often it is the only acceptable mode of communicating uncomfortable or difficult truths to others. A sense of humor is one of the surest signs of balance and perspective in ordinary life — a sign that someone understands that life is meant to be enjoyed and that we can find something funny even in our deepest foibles, mistakes, and misfortunes. We all like to laugh, and we all enjoy those who make us laugh; they become dear to us. Laughter is evidence of *real* joy, a divine gift.

Breathe in happily and breathe out happily.
If you are a Christian, breathe in Christ, breathe in God;
if you are a nonbeliever, just breathe in one, two.
This is the first step in awareness.

— Sulak Sivaraksa

Breathing consciously — with attention, intention, and determination — is the first step toward awareness of what is. Sulak Sivaraksa, a lay Buddhist thinker and activist, is founder of the International Network of Engaged Buddhists, which views Buddhism as a spirituality that requires active engagement with the world and its politics. Yet his practice begins and ends with the breath. The Christian, Jewish, and Sufi mystic knows that every breath we take is a participation in the Divine breathing, or *spiration*. Jesus is said to have communicated the Holy Spirit to his disciples by breathing on them. And all of creation, in all universes, is breathed into being by God. Breath is Spirit, is the Divine, or an indication of its presence. The breath carries the reality of the Divine, and it is a vehicle of its transmission.

*At the end of life, when someone has lived a life
with consciousness and they look back on it,
the questions are simple: "Did I live fully?" and,
more than anything else, "Did I love well?"*

— Jack Kornfield

There is no escape from authenticity! Buddhist teacher and writer Jack Kornfield brings us to the essential questions of human life, and each one of us will ask ourselves these same questions in our own way and in our own time. So much of awareness has to do with the sensitivity required in understanding how to achieve fulfillment. It takes awareness to really love selflessly, to be free of ego-cherishing. To live life with awareness is to live each moment with real sensitivity and receptivity to others, their sufferings and need. To live fully is to be aware of the opportunities to be compassionate and loving toward others. To love well is to love unselfishly and to strive to be ever more inclusive, extending one's care even to those with whom we would not ordinarily associate. It is to be spontaneously open and receptive to those we meet who may need us in some way. In this sense, life is a school where we are learning how to love more authentically and more comprehensively, including more and more people into our circle.

[205]

Both denial and hope show us
where our attachments are.

— Terry Tempest Williams

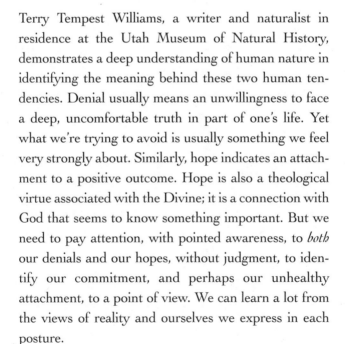

Terry Tempest Williams, a writer and naturalist in residence at the Utah Museum of Natural History, demonstrates a deep understanding of human nature in identifying the meaning behind these two human tendencies. Denial usually means an unwillingness to face a deep, uncomfortable truth in part of one's life. Yet what we're trying to avoid is usually something we feel very strongly about. Similarly, hope indicates an attachment to a positive outcome. Hope is also a theological virtue associated with the Divine; it is a connection with God that seems to know something important. But we need to pay attention, with pointed awareness, to *both* our denials and our hopes, without judgment, to identify our commitment, and perhaps our unhealthy attachment, to a point of view. We can learn a lot from the views of reality and ourselves we express in each posture.

Hope proves man deathless.

— Herman Melville

True hope, which is theologically grounded or in touch with the Divine, gives certitude. In this quote from the great novel *Moby Dick*, writer Herman Melville shows that he understood that hope carries with it a certain knowledge intuited in the act of hoping itself. It is not like the rootless hopes of people and their ambitions, like politicians running for office who believe they have a chance to win even when the odds are against them. Such hope isn't based on anything real, but rather is simply wishful thinking. Genuine hope is emotional certitude — a certainty that unites with emotional conviction — that we will achieve ultimate well-being beyond this world of impermanence. This hope has a transcendent source just as it has a transcendent destiny.

Fear's contagious, but so is courage.

— Betty Williams

Betty Williams, a peace activist who shared the 1976 Nobel Peace Prize with Mairead Corrigan Maguire, speaks a truth here she knows from her own experience. In their work to end the conflict between Protestants and Catholics in Northern Ireland, she and Maguire had to battle against their own fear and the fear of the members of their respective communities. Fear is the easiest thing in the world; it's cheap and widespread. Tyrants and oppressors count on fear's contagion to dominate others. But if one person steps forward and summons courage, his or her courage becomes equally contagious, spreading to others and becoming a movement. Just as it took supreme courage for these two extraordinary women to confront the tragedy of communal conflict and lead their communities to a vision of the possibility of peace, it takes courage in our lives to confront the challenges that are given to us. But after one person makes the first courageous step, others will follow.

*Wisdom consists in doing the next thing
that you have to do...doing it with your whole heart
and finding delight in doing it.
And the delight is the sense of the sacred.*

— Helen Luke

Helen Luke is a British Jungian who writes about the inner life, symbol, and story. She writes that wisdom is knowing what is required of us. We often know, sometimes unconsciously, what is next for us when we live our life consciously, accepting opportunities and challenges as they arise. Each of us will often know what we have to do, and if we do it with understanding and a willing heart, we will embrace it with real delight and joy. This joy is the presence of the sacred. Yet it takes great clarity of mind and heart to know what to do next, to have this kind of practical wisdom. Wisdom of this sort is the fruit of an inner life and an availability to others.

Man has no Body distinct from his Soul:
for that called Body is a portion of soul
discerned by the Five Senses,
the chief inlets of Soul in this age.

— William Blake

The great English mystical poet William Blake grasped what the mystic sages of India have always known: The body exists within the soul, and the soul is another way of speaking about consciousness. The body is not distinct or separate from consciousness. It exists because of awareness and has no life in its own right. The body is saturated by the soul, by the vivifying principle that defines the nature of the body and how soul and body interact in this world. The senses are portals to the soul of the perceiving person who looks out in awareness toward all things on the path of experience. The body is, in Blake's vision, a manifestation of the soul, an external concretization of its embodied state, but a more visual, tangible aspect of the soul's reality.

We shall not cease from exploration
and the end of all our exploring
will be to arrive where we started
and know the place for the first time. .

— T. S. Eliot

This English-American poet, in one of his more mystical utterances, speaks of all our explorations of experience — be it of the inner life, nature, the cosmos,
relationships, creativity, knowledge, poetry, music, or
art. In all we are searching for Ultimate Reality, the
Divine Ground from which all our lives derive. Eliot
refers both to the perennial quest and the return to the
Godhead from whence we are derived and to which we
will return at the end of our lives. Returning to the
Divine Ground after having been awakened by experience, we understand it for the first time with much
greater clarity, depth, and joy.

Exultation is the going of an inland soul to sea,
past the houses — past the headlands —
into deep Eternity....

— Emily Dickinson

Emily Dickinson's profound sensitivity allowed her poetry to express ideas beyond the normal range of perception. She felt things that escape most people. Drawing on the metaphor of rivers to the sea, she evokes the return to the Blessed One. Through ecstatic exultation, the soul breaks out of its isolation. It passes from an "inland soul" to one that has entered into the Divine Sea, passing all the familiar objects along the way to Eternal Reality. Joy is a Divine attribute, one of the many gifts that God gives us, and it has the power to lead us more deeply into God's inner life. Spiritual exultation is grace at work in us. Divine exultation is a treasure God gives us in the course of our interior life, the fruit of a balance between Divine Grace and our effort.

We shall never find God anywhere
so perfectly, so fruitfully, and so truly
as in retirement and in the wilderness.

— Johann Tauler

Johann Tauler (1300–1361), a Rhineland mystic in the tradition of Dominican friar Meister Eckhart, was an intense introvert. He was convinced, through his own inner experience, that withdrawal from the world is necessary to make possible the fullness of union with God. He was totally committed to a contemplative life that emphasized complete retirement from society and external obligations. It is not that God is less present in the hustle and bustle of the world, but that the world obscures the Divine with its emphasis on endless distraction. In the stillness and the silence of our will we discover the Divine. The wilderness, where we can definitely find the Divine, is not only the earthly wilderness, but also Eckhart's mystical notion of the wilderness of the Godhead. Are you ready to make this withdrawal and enter into the great wilderness of the Godhead?

You have made us for yourself, Oh God,
and our hearts are restless till they find their rest in you.

— St. Augustine

St. Augustine begins his great autobiographical work, *The Confessions,* with this prayer. Augustine knew the constitution of human nature: that ultimate happiness is only possible in union with God. Everything else makes us restless. Nothing can fulfill us quite as God can. He knew at once the destiny of the human in intimacy with the Divine as well as the weaknesses of human nature. Augustine realized that most humans are not up to the task of seeking wholehearted intimacy with God and rest in him, the rest of fulfilled contemplation. We were made by God and for God, Augustine reminds us in this evocation. He reveals the vocation of human life as a journey into the mystery of the Divine Presence. This journey grows more profound the more we enter into a relationship with and surrender to God. This is the mystic path.

Our lives begin to end the day we become
silent about things that matter.
— Martin Luther King, Jr.

This sobering adage by one of the great prophetic figures of the twentieth century spurs us on in our commitment to justice, hope, and dedicated action. It's easy to
fall into a pattern of acquiescence and silence, particularly when we are comfortable and our daily needs are
being met. To speak out and take a firm stand against
injustice and oppression is an act that exposes us to danger and maybe even death, as was the case with King
and M. K. Gandhi. Of course, as Shakespeare observed,
"Fear doth make cowards of us all," and perhaps our
fear fuels our silence. But silence is a tenuous refuge,
one that doesn't really protect us. Sooner or later, injustice reaches us all. Dr. King's statement is a warning
that we need to guard ourselves against a kind of moral
death that befalls us if we aren't vigilant against indifference and fear.

[215]

*Not through much learning is the Atman reached,
not through the intellect and sacred teaching. It is reached
by the chosen of him — because they choose him.
To his chosen the Atman reveals his glory.*

— Katha Upanishad

In this passage, the Katha Upanishad offers us a universal spiritual truth that we find in many traditions, including Christianity. The Divine Reality reveals itself not to the person who seeks it in books. Nor does it manifest itself to the intellect, which seeks it in philosophical or theological study and reflection. It certainly cannot be grasped by scientific method and analysis. In fact, it is not possible to connect with the Divine One through any activity of the mind, other than prayer or meditation, which are really *inactions* of the mind. The Atman, the Eternal Self, chooses us if we choose it. We are told in the Gospel, "Many are called, but few are chosen." Actually, everyone is called, and the few that are chosen are the ones who choose God. To make this choice for God, or for the Atman, means a total surrender to that ultimate reality; the Divine then takes a giant step toward us. Are you prepared to choose the Divine? If so, you will experience God's choosing of you.

[216]

Commend what you do to Yahweh,
and what you plan will be achieved.

— Proverbs

⁓

This bit of wisdom from Proverbs 16:3 tells us that if our plans are conceived in relationship to Yahweh — that is if we selflessly surrender our plans to God and dedicate them to him — then they will be realized. Such dedication of our work to God is like a consecration. When our motivation arises from a purity of intention, our plans take on a singular power. Do you make your plans with God in mind? Are they motivated by love and a simple dedication to good?

Blessed are the poor in spirit,
for theirs is the kingdom of heaven.
— Gospel of Matthew

These powerful words from the New Testament (Matthew 5:3) form the first of the beatitudes, the charter of the kingdom of heaven. When Jesus tells us that "the poor in spirit" are blessed, he is not referring to people with little money. While many of the poor are indeed blessed, it isn't due to their poverty but to a condition of their hearts, to the fact that they are poor in spirit. To be poor in spirit, or in one's heart, is to be free of selfishness, guile, and ulterior motive. Poverty of spirit is actually simplicity of heart and mind. It is freedom from all the manipulations that a complicated heart can attach itself to when forgetting its inwardly free and open deeper nature. The poor in spirit have docile hearts, and this docility makes them receptive to the Divine will. Let us search for this poverty of spirit.

In the name of Allah, the Beneficent, the Merciful.

— The Qur'an

This is the opening verse of the Qur'an, found in sura 1:1. It is the dedication of all things to Allah and the identification of his two most important attributes in relationship to us. It is the recognition of his sovereignty over all things. As evidenced by the Islamic practice of turning toward Mecca five times a day to pray, remembrance of God is the most crucial point and focus for Muslims. This opening is the prophet Muhammad's testimony to his remembrance of Allah and the Qur'an's way of guiding other Muslims to similarly remember him. Allah is all merciful and compassionate. God's compassion and mercy are infinite, comprehensive, inclusive, and profoundly effective in the lives of those who are touched by God's grace.

Pain is often the precursor of change.

— Mel Gibson

As I was working on this book, actor and director Mel Gibson's film *The Passion of the Christ* was stirring intense controversy. During a conversation with television journalist Diane Sawyer, in the midst of discussing the film's unrelenting focus on Christ's pain during the crucifixion, Gibson spoke of his own struggle with addiction to alcohol and drugs — his own inner pain, anguish, and suffering, as well as the pain, anguish, and suffering he brought to his family and friends. As he neared the decision to fight his addictions, he realized that any substantial change in his life toward sobriety, sanity, health, and spiritual well-being would involve more suffering, pain, misunderstanding, self-doubt, and frustration. But this kind of suffering — steps in the process of being healed — are salutary. In a very real sense, addiction is the first step in a long path, involving confronting and overcoming it, that eventually leads to spiritual transformation.

[220]

In wilderness is the preservation of the world.
— Henry David Thoreau

⁓

Henry David Thoreau knew that human well-being, indeed the well-being of all creatures, depends on a positive connection with nature, and specifically with untrammeled wilderness. Wilderness, the *freedom* of the natural world, calls humankind back to the enduring sanity and intelligence of wild things. Only by developing and maintaining a healthy relationship with nature will we survive as a species. A healthy relationship is one that enhances rather than impedes the earth's functioning, that finds new ways to live in harmony with all species. It is only in the reality and resource of the wilderness that humans will discover the wisdom we need to survive.

The family that prays together, stays together.

— Irish proverb

One troubling problem for many families is that they lack a common spiritual agreement. I believe this problem stems from not sharing any spiritual practice. By thinking creatively, a family can find a spiritual practice that reflects diversity of spiritual belief. Maybe it means meditation, or a practice of silence before meals, or the saying of grace — whatever grace means for each family member. Negotiating difficult family crises often requires a spiritual relationship. When a family or people who love each other perform some prayer or meditation together, they are in a stronger position to weather storms. Shared spiritual practice becomes a precious reservoir to draw upon in difficult times.

[222]

*Who can trace the invisible path of the person
who soars in the sky of liberation, the infinite Void
without beginning, whose passions are peace,
and over whom pleasures have no power?*

— The Dhammapada

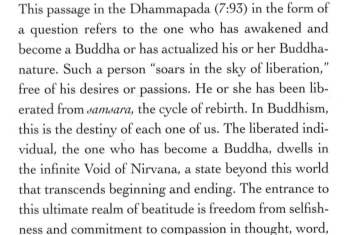

This passage in the Dhammapada (7:93) in the form of a question refers to the one who has awakened and become a Buddha or has actualized his or her Buddha-nature. Such a person "soars in the sky of liberation," free of his desires or passions. He or she has been liberated from *samsara,* the cycle of rebirth. In Buddhism, this is the destiny of each one of us. The liberated individual, the one who has become a Buddha, dwells in the infinite Void of Nirvana, a state beyond this world that transcends beginning and ending. The entrance to this ultimate realm of beatitude is freedom from selfishness and commitment to compassion in thought, word, and action.

Learn from the past —
don't wear it like a yoke around your neck.

— Cogitor Reticulus

Here's another piece of science fiction wisdom — this one from the character Cogitor Reticulus found in Brian Herbert and Kevin Anderson's novel *Dune: The Butlerian Jihad*. Rather than following the lessons they've discerned from past experience, some people, and even nations, become trapped by them. The past should not determine the future; wisdom culled from our experiences should guide the present and future course in a spirit of continuity. We should strive to genuinely learn from our own past mistakes, being very careful not to repeat them, shrugging off both past humiliations and victories, but remaining alert and open to the possibilities and opportunities the future holds.

When we listen to the "inner voice,"
the place we come to eventually is silence.

— Dorothy Fadiman

⌒

As we've seen earlier, silence is one of the places where the Divine dwells. As visionary filmmaker Dorothy Fadiman states, every artistic achievement — be it painting, sculpture, writing, music, dancing, or film-making — begins with listening to our intuitive inner voice, which leads us eventually to silence, the stillness of the Divine Presence. The more we listen to the Divine's voice within the depths of our own being, the more it will lead us into the silence, "the language of God," as Father Thomas Keating has called it. Everything is present in silence, where the creative spirit of our individual being unites with that vast storehouse of insight, connection, clarity, vision, and infinite wisdom that springs from the Divine.

To bring the four energies together in the moment —
physical, intellectual, spiritual, and emotional —
is the fundamental artistic act.
That is where the joy arises.

— Dick Richards

Creativity cannot simply engage the intellectual; the resulting work of art would be too abstract. It cannot result only from spiritual energy, or the art might lack a connection with physical reality, the body, the world, or the clarity and compelling power of an idea. As Dick Richards says in his helpful book *Artful Work,* the mature work integrates physical, intellectual, spiritual, and emotional factors. And when these four essential energies work together in the life of the artist, the creative moment arrives, a source of immense joy and true bliss.

*We experience forgiveness daily, from the source
of our creation and for ourselves. We also need
to be able to forgive, because if we don't, we put our foot
right down on the hose of our life force.*

— Sue Patton Thoele

Often when we face the decision to forgive, we fall under the illusion that the act involves giving something up, that somehow we will lose something of ourselves if we decide to forgive. In reality, forgiveness can only help us. As author Sue Thoele conveys so accurately with the analogy of a garden hose, we choke off our own vitality, our life force, when we withhold our forgiveness. This life force is actually love itself, which flows in all directions in the act of forgiving.

[227]

*You don't get much out of passive consumption
of pleasure, compared to enjoyment
that is active, creative, and self-directive.*
— Mihaly Csikszentmihalyi

Mihaly Csikszentmihalyi, author of *Creativity: Flow and
the Psychology of Discovery and Invention,* is a University of
Chicago professor of psychology celebrated for his
insights into what he calls "flow" — the experience
of the creative act, where everything comes together
and the artist loses his or her sense of self in the act of
doing. Flow is something we all experience, and it is far
more profound and enjoyable than passive pleasure.
True creativity engages the whole person. This height-
ened state of enjoyment often has a passionate purpose
related to the individual. Ultimately this is a mystical
experience, one where our typical thoughts and dis-
tracting preoccupations give way to a glimpse of something larger.

[228]

Sustainability [refers to] a society in which fulfilling our needs of today does not jeopardize the chances of future generations.

— Fritjof Capra

Sustainability is really a spiritual notion, one that strikes at the heart of our actions and responsibilities. Fortunately it is also a notion that more and more fields of discipline are embracing. Fritjof Capra, the visionary physicist and author of numerous books including *Web of Life* and *The Tao of Physics*, defines this idea, which affects us all and requires a positive response from us in the form of individual and collective responsibility. Our society as it stands is fundamentally unsustainable. We simply don't consider the welfare of future generations in our current actions. The entire model of the corporation and public ownership of those corporations emphasizes short-term profit at the cost of nearly everything else. We have ruthlessly pursued our needs and pleasures as if there were no tomorrow. Even though it has also become important in ecology, economics, and political theory, sustainability is really a wise lesson from the Native American tribes, who factor the welfare of future generations into every decision. It is the wisdom of the earth.

Attitude is everything.
How you understand something
makes all the difference in whether
your experience is happiness or suffering.

— Christine Longaker

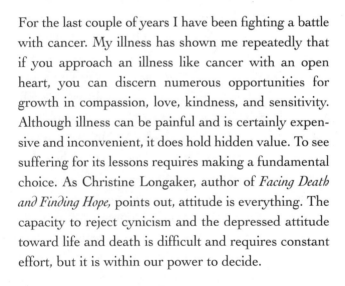

For the last couple of years I have been fighting a battle with cancer. My illness has shown me repeatedly that if you approach an illness like cancer with an open heart, you can discern numerous opportunities for growth in compassion, love, kindness, and sensitivity. Although illness can be painful and is certainly expensive and inconvenient, it does hold hidden value. To see suffering for its lessons requires making a fundamental choice. As Christine Longaker, author of *Facing Death and Finding Hope,* points out, attitude is everything. The capacity to reject cynicism and the depressed attitude toward life and death is difficult and requires constant effort, but it is within our power to decide.

*I make sense of the world by borrowing what I can
from people to whom I listen.
Life is a continuing course in Adult Education.*

— Bill Moyers

Celebrated broadcast journalist Bill Moyers has followed his curiosity through several careers. A deputy director of the Peace Corps and special assistant to President Lyndon Johnson, Moyers has for the last twenty-five years focused the television lens on people who have a lot to teach, from mythologist Joseph Campbell to biblical scholars to physicians exploring the link between mind and body. As Moyers reminds us, we are continually learning from one another; this is how knowledge advances and how we all make sense of our existence. Learning is a community enterprise, and our education is an ongoing journey. Let us each listen more carefully, more devoutly, to each other, never letting the world quash our curiosity for new ideas. Together we'll gain a much better grasp of this life and our world.

A plant can't live without roots. Your soul is your root.

— Yogi Bhajan

⌒

Employing a horticultural metaphor, Yogi Bhajan, the spiritual leader of thousands of Sikhs in North America, stresses the importance of attaining harmony with your soul — learning who you really are in the permanent sense. Being true to yourself, in your deepest nature as you arise in God, is essential. Just as a tree, a bush, or a flower cannot live without roots, we cannot live without being firmly established in our souls. The soul should also be nourished and cared for, just as a gardener nurtures the growth and well-being of his garden. Prayer, meditation, kindness, and love are ways to nourish the soul, the root of our being.

Compassion for yourself translates into
compassion for others.

— Suki Jay Munsell

Just as charity begins at home, compassion begins with oneself. Suki Jay Munsell, founder and director of the Transformations Institute, highlights something very basic in our growth to greater compassion. We have to see our own value as people; we have to understand that we are intrinsically lovable. We have to recognize our essential goodness, the goodness that reflects the eternal goodness of God. Being compassionate with ourselves is how we learn compassion toward everyone else, every other sentient being. How can we hope to be truly aware of others and their needs if we don't really accept ourselves?

Life has a vital sonic dimension that colors our moods and sentiments, our joys and fears, our love and pain.

— Russill Paul

⌒

Music and sound are intrinsic to life, and we would be greatly impoverished without them. Just consider how music adds to a movie, bringing life to the screen and engaging our emotions. Life's "vital sonic dimension," which Russill Paul writes about in *The Yoga of Sound*, also connects us with the Divine Presence in all things and beyond all things. It plays a significant role in the development of our inner capacities, particularly sacred music specifically composed to accompany spiritual practice — whether it's Gregorian chant, Indian classical ragas or mantras, or the deep tones of Tibetan Buddhist horns and chanting. Music also becomes a symbolic vehicle to express the depth of our relationships with one another.

We should listen with one ear closed
so that we can listen to ourselves
and the other ear open
so that we can listen to each other.

— Maria Suarez

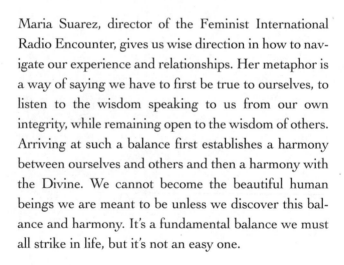

Maria Suarez, director of the Feminist International Radio Encounter, gives us wise direction in how to navigate our experience and relationships. Her metaphor is a way of saying we have to first be true to ourselves, to listen to the wisdom speaking to us from our own integrity, while remaining open to the wisdom of others. Arriving at such a balance first establishes a harmony between ourselves and others and then a harmony with the Divine. We cannot become the beautiful human beings we are meant to be unless we discover this balance and harmony. It's a fundamental balance we must all strike in life, but it's not an easy one.

*The Ultimate Truth is so simple; it is nothing more
than being in one's natural, original state.*

— Sri Ramana Maharshi

Sri Ramana Maharshi (1879–1950), the silent seer of
Arunachala in Tamil Nadu, South India, was one of modern India's greatest saints. He describes here the experience of *advaita,* or nonduality, the reality of a unified
mind and consciousness, the experience of the eternally abiding Self present in all of us. This is our natural and original state. When we experience our original
state, our natural connection with the Divine, we become aware that we *are* this ultimate reality expressed
through individual consciousness. We are part of the
Ocean of Being, though within this unity there are endless distinctions of individual consciousnesses. Can you
look beyond the ego or false self, which is impermanent,
and see who you are in the final sense? Meditation is a
way to discover the original, natural state of nonduality.

Every time we suffer, we grow.

— Ram Dass

Ram Dass is certainly no stranger to suffering. He first experienced psychological turmoil and misunderstanding when he made a break from his academic life at Harvard, where he was a research professor in psychology. He underwent deep psychological changes in his awakening to India's mystical tradition through his guru, Neem Karoli Baba, as well as in his exposure to living conditions in India. More recently, he experienced intense physical suffering after enduring a stroke. These challenges, and many others, granted him considerable wisdom about the nature and value of suffering in transforming us. Suffering has a way of opening our hearts and putting us in touch with our compassionate nature. I know this from my own experience with cancer. You cannot avoid growth if your heart is open. Suffering teaches us to love and to be kind, compassionate, and sensitive to the struggles of others. It is the greatest means of enlarging our perspective.

The crisis is in our consciousness, not in the world.

— J. Krishnamurti

All around us we see crisis and conflict. But Krishna-murti had hold of the essential truth of the Indian mystical and philosophical tradition: that the locus of reality lies in consciousness, that there is nothing outside this consciousness, and that this consciousness, in an ultimate sense, is Divine. There is really no "outside." Everything is happening within; everything is processed in the mind. Every problem we encounter starts in the mind, in its distortions and misunderstandings. We glare out at the world, resenting it for controlling our lives, when actually reality lies within.

[238]

The spiritual journey, or process itself,
is what Jesus called the Kingdom of God....
If we are on the journey, we are in the Kingdom.

— Thomas Keating

In his wonderful masterpiece *Intimacy with God,* Father Thomas Keating reveals to us a subtlety of the Gospel to which Jesus often referred in his teachings. This subtlety is at work throughout his parables, and it could radically shake the understanding of religious belief held by many practitioners. If we are living the spiritual life with dedication, persistence, and joy, we are fully alive and present in the Kingdom of God. Being in the Kingdom of God, the Kingdom of Heaven, requires that we follow an inner journey in which our relationship with God is the centerpiece of our life and the destiny of the journey itself. Being in the Kingdom is a commitment to prayer, especially the mystical prayer the Christian tradition calls contemplation. It doesn't matter if we stumble on the way. What does matter is that we get up and keep on the path. We may often struggle with God, but throughout it all, if we love him, we will reside in his kingdom.

Whoever does not understand the language of poetry
should not be allowed to touch the Bible
or any other sacred text.

— Ron Miller

⌒

Biblical and religious scholar Ron Miller suggests that
the poetic dimension is an essential part of communicating the Divine. Christianity has long recognized that
there are four levels of meaning in the Bible: the literal,
moral, typological, and anagogic, or mystical. The typological views certain biblical figures as representing
certain qualities: Mary the generous heart and Joseph
faithfulness and obedience to God. The problem is that
many people glibly interpret in literal terms something
meant poetically, or metaphorically, like the Red Sea
parting. When we strive to understand the multiple
levels of meaning in scripture, the symbolic and meta-
phorical, we come away with a much more powerful
sense of spirituality and a greater respect for religion.

[240]

The news we hear is full of grief for the future,
but the real news inside here is there's no news at all.

— Rumi

Rumi's age was full of the same challenges we face today: the problem of extremism, the gap between the haves and the have-nots, divided communities, religious wars, and the ever-present task of building peace. Like ours, Rumi's future was clouded by a bombardment of disturbing news. While the external world is replete with such news, the *real* news is the inner journey. The demands on us are the same, and nothing ever changes in what God expects of us. He wants us to surrender to him in love, and he wants our total attention. The Divine is ever calling us in every aspect of our lives. It is a call to intimacy with God.

The master observes the world but trusts his inner vision.
He allows things to come and go.
His heart is open as the sky.

— Tao Te Ching

This wonderful and meaningful passage from Stephen
Mitchell's translation of the Tao Te Ching describes the
nature and vision of the sage. He watches and observes
but is loyal to his inner vision. He practices nonattach-
ment and is inwardly free. He observes everything but
trusts what he knows. He lets nature take its course and
watches as people, events, and the seasons come and
go. He has an inner spaciousness that embraces everything. He lets things be; he acts by not acting, not mani-
pulating others, processes, nature, or reality. In the rare
moments when he acts, he acts deliberately for unselfish
reasons. His inner vision, as spacious as the universe,
guides him in all things. He follows the way of Heaven,
which is also the way of Nature, the Tao, the Divine.

*You find your soul and your destiny by responding to
the world's call to you. That's how you find yourself.*

— Thomas Moore

The way to truly find ourselves is to let go of our selfish aims and embrace the need of others expressed
through the call of the world. Only by becoming a ser-
vant to the world — through whatever message stirs
our hearts to act — do we discover our souls and their
purpose in this reality and beyond. Thomas Moore,
who has distinguished himself as a master of the science and art of the soul, is pointing out here a wisdom
found in every tradition. Our souls are interconnected
with every other soul in the divine reality. The roots of
our identity span the infinity of God, who invites us to
discover this vast community beyond the ego. The way
in is through selfless service to others, even if it's only
prayer and simple acts of kindness and love.

[243]

There's a lot we can do in the fast lane —
we can grow and we can expand.
But we cannot deepen, and we cannot integrate
our experiences, unless we slow down.

— Angeles Arrien

Deepening and integration require contemplation. In our more lucid moments, we all grasp this fundamental truth that anthropologist Angeles Arrien, author of *Signs of Life*, emphasizes here. If we are always racing around, we won't develop our relationship with the Divine. Contemplation needs time, a kind of holy leisure, if it is to unfold and blossom. Contemplation is one of the best ways to achieve access to depth and to bring about final integration, in which we discover the roots of our being. When we deepen and find integration of our most important experiences, we also find the common ground with all other sentient beings. To enter into this depth of realization, we must slow down and make contemplation a singular priority in our lives.

The hurrier I go, the behinder I get.

— New England proverb

This folksy bit of practical wisdom from New England fits well with the preceding advice from Angeles Arrien. Constantly rushing discourages authentic behavior. It is the opposite of compassion, kindness, love, and sensitivity, and more important, it is the enemy of being present, both to the moment and to others. To be truly present, we have to take our time, whether we are looking at the task at hand, which we can then do with good intention and efficiency, or listening to the people around us, who we can respond to authentically and appropriately. And of course when we're in our hurried state, we are unable to attend to spiritual practice. Again, contemplation takes time. Decide to make time for prayer, meditation, and quiet in your life. Allow yourself to slow down and be present to others and to the miracle of the present moment.

O friend, the heart is the dwelling of eternal mysteries.
Make it not the home of fleeting fancies; waste not
the treasure of your precious life in the employment
with this swiftly passing world. You come from the world
of holiness; do not bind your heart to the earth.

— Baha'u'llah

This mystical prophet, who arose in Islam in Iran to found the Baha'i faith, alerts us to keep our hearts and minds free of the corrupting influences of the world. Keep your heart fixed on the eternal, the permanent, what does not pass away. The Divine is present in our beings, our hearts, and intellects. The eternal mysteries and truths are operating in us, and we must keep ourselves as vessels of the Spirit, clear of the world's polluting illusions, its impermanent projects, fantasies, fashions, and all that falls short of compassion, love, kindness, and sensitivity. We are citizens of Heaven, Baha'u'llah reminds us, so we must not bind ourselves to this world.

[246]

Whatever you did to the least of my brethren,
you did unto me.

— Gospel of Matthew

What ultimately counts is the openness of our hearts and our receptivity to the suffering of others. This passage from Matthew's Gospel (25:40) represents Jesus' teaching about the Last Judgment, where salvation will depend on how we respond to the vulnerable in our lives. Love in action holds an absolute place in the Gospel. Love gives us the sensitivity to see and hear others and compels us to be aware, to respond to what we see and hear. When we can look beyond the surface, and are able to see and feel the demands of love in every moment, then we are in the Kingdom of Heaven. In every situation, the Spirit is calling us to love, to understand everything with the heart. Love calls to us in the homeless, the hungry, the stranger, the prisoner, and the abandoned child, the forgotten elderly, the ill and the dying, the unloved and unwanted. Do you hear its call?

Within the city of Brahman, which is the body,
there is the heart, and within the heart there is a little house.
This house has the shape of a lotus,
and within it dwells that which is to be
sought after, inquired about, and realized.

— Chandogya Upanishad

This passage (8.1) is from Chandogya, one of the old-est Upanishads, composed around 1700 B.C.E. but with an oral tradition extending back to at least 2700 B.C.E. It contains a metaphor of enormous scope, incorporat-ing an incredible panorama of reality that involves the totality of what is. The "city of Brahman" is a Hindu parallel to the Christian understanding of the body as the Mystical Body of Christ. The little house or shrine, in the form of a lotus, is the locus of all reality. Every-thing is present there. God is within us — the universe, others, everything — and we dwell in the Divine's con-sciousness. Everything is found in our consciousness, and our consciousness subsists in God's.

[248]

As long as space remains,
as long as sentient beings remain,
until then, may I too remain
and dispel the miseries of the world.

— Shantideva

This wonderful passage is His Holiness the Dalai Lama's favorite and comes from a section of *Shantideva's Guide to the Bodhisattva's Way of Life* called Generating the Mind for Enlightenment. Shantideva was an eighth-century Tibetan spiritual master, and his book has been very influential in defining the precise Buddhist principles of the *bodhisattva,* a being who puts off his or her own liberation and entrance into *paranirvana,* the ultimate state, until all sentient beings are liberated. There are literally millions of these Christ-like beings on the earth, many from traditions other than Buddhism. The *bodhisattva* way is of selflessness and altruism, the path of the saint. In generating the mind for enlightenment, the aspiring *bodhisattva* must have the motivation to give of himself for the sake of others.

Everything is linked with everything else;
so divine essence is below as well as above,
in heaven and on earth. There is nothing else.

— Moses de Leon

The Spanish Jewish mystic Moses de Leon (d. 1305) was the probable author of *Zohar: The Book of Splendor,* a central kabbalistic text in Jewish mysticism. In the above passage, which might at first be confused with the teachings of an enlightened Buddhist master, he refers to the great chain of being that Divine unity provides, connecting all beings together in God. The inner nature or essence of each thing or sentient being is united to every other in God and through God. The Divine essence is immanently present in each being and in the laws of the universe. In every atom, electron, star, galaxy, and creature — in the cosmos as a whole — the Divine reality is the immanent ground and transcendent destiny of all beings. Do you feel your connection with the Divine, how intimately it connects everything in our lives?

The successive movement of yin and yang
constitutes what is called the Way (Tao).
What issues from it is good, and that which brings it
to completion is the individual nature.

— Alan Watts

Alan Watts, the brilliant Western popularizer of Eastern meditation and thought, indicates how the creative, balancing forces of yin and yang are part of how the Tao works in nature, cosmos, life, and being. Our individual natures are manifestations of the unfolding movement of the yin and yang principles, which in turn encompass and represent every opposite that exists. Yang represents light; yin dark. Yang represents male; yin female. Each opposite produces the other, and in their entirety they encompass the Tao, or the Way. Yet they are more than just a play of principles; they uncover the ultimate truth of human nature.

Breathing teaches you everything you need to know —
right under your nose.

— Gay Hendricks

⌒⌒⌒

There is ultimate knowledge, or access to it, in the simple act of breathing. Breathing is so intimate to each one of us, almost as close to us as our thoughts. Because it is mechanically second nature to our bodies, we often lose sight of its real importance. In *Conscious Breathing*, Gay Hendricks explores how being consciously attentive to our breathing allows us to gain some control over our lives, greatly improve our health, and cope with all the stress from our fast-paced existence and the demands of our culture. As a Christian monk, I find conscious breathing a quick way to still the mind, so that I can become more attuned to and aware of God. Of course, in Hindu and Buddhist forms of meditation, the breath is the central focus of all practice. Whether we treat it as a gateway to God or a way to relax, attention to our breath is crucial to spiritual practice.

[252]

*We're the first culture to create so much isolation
for human beings. Now we are moving back toward
community — because we need it to happen.*

— Gay Luce

⁓

My spiritual mentor Bede Griffiths often remarked that
it was in community that humanity would find its salvation, not in the nuclear family. As Gay Luce, the author
of *Body Time*, observes here, our culture has excelled in
promoting the possibility of isolation and privacy for
people. While this has allowed us great creativity, it has
ripped apart our social fabric. The luxury of expansive
houses surrounded by acres of lawn and filled with iso-
lating forms of entertainment such as television and the
Internet has cut us off from our neighbors. Now we are
seeking greater contacts with a life-giving community
with whom we can share what is really important in our
lives. Successful communities are often united in deep
commitments, whether to a spiritual vision or a way of
life, but we have to work hard for our communities to
be diverse and tolerant. True community includes those
we disagree with. Community building, whether on our
block or across national or cultural divides, is the great
work of our new millennium.

Community will be humanity's salvation.

— Bede Griffiths

⌒

Father Bede Griffiths was born in Britain but lived in India for more than forty years. After he became an icon of interspiritual thought, he was taken to the United Nations in 1979 to speak with world leaders. As he was leaving the building, he looked back and remarked: "The renewal of the world will not come through that organization, but from something more rooted in the earth itself." Later he clarified his remark, revealing that it would come from a rediscovery and recovery of community, as Gay Luce intimated in the previous quotation. Father Bede had in mind small, manageable communities with a contemplative vision and practice as the focus of their commitment to live together. Their membership would include married and single people, the elderly, children, the poor and vulnerable. Communities would not be afraid of the poor but would make a place for them. Have you ever lived in a community other than your family? Do you have the generosity and the courage to experiment in such a human adventure?

*Medicine really is an art, not a science, however much
doctors try to pretend they are being scientific.*

— Dr. Andrew Weil

⁓

You aren't likely to hear Andrew Weil's insight mentioned in medical school, the doctor's office, or a hospi-
tal. Doctors typically show complete confidence in
scientific certainty, but there is a lot more to healing, as
Dr. Weil, who champions a more holistic approach to
health, highlights here. When we approach healing as
an art, we realize it requires the use of intuition, engaged compassion, tremendous openness, the capacity
to be amazed, and an acknowledgment that the mind
and its beliefs have a powerful effect on illness. The scientific approach cannot guarantee health. Our extraordinary technological advances and scientific knowledge
must be balanced with a humble acknowledgment that
the health of our bodies is a wonderful mystery.

Every important change in our society, for the good,
at least, has taken place because of popular pressure —
pressure from below, from the great mass of the people.

— Edward Abbey

Author of *One Life at a Time, Please,* the great iconoclastic naturalist Edward Abbey identifies a basic principle of social, economic, political, cultural, and spiritual change: the necessity of what the eighteenth-century Quakers called "speaking truth to power." The pressure of conscience and integrity often sparks substantial change in individual lives, and when those individuals are brought together they can effect societal change. Mass pressure, with the inspiration of a few great leaders, can bring about substantial change, as we saw with the Civil Rights movement in the sixties. People power, the open secret of mass movements, is an inexhaustible resource. People power may yet emerge as the most potent force on earth, the best vehicle for far-reaching change on our planet, but it is up against the powerful foe of moneyed interests desperately clinging to the status quo. If we are to create a universal civilization with a heart, a global society that works for everyone, then we need to tap the masses of humankind to light the spark. Would you be part of a people's movement for change? You are needed.

Blessed are the meek, for they shall inherit the earth.

— Gospel of Matthew

Through this passage of Matthew's Gospel (5:5), Jesus singles out the attribute of mildness of nature as a characteristic of one who is a member of the Kingdom of God. The way of meekness and nonviolence, of gentleness and patience, will ultimately prevail, and those who are committed to meekness will be the heirs of the planet. The values of this beatitude oppose the easy path of violence, vengeance, and aggression. It holds out the hope that in the long run peace and nonviolence will prevail. Consider well this wise teaching of Christ. It holds a secret for all of us.

Utopia is never produced through educational reform at the institutional level. Utopia resides in subtle, one-on-one relationships between individuals.

— Robert Fuller

Robert Fuller, president emeritus of Oberlin College and chairperson of InterNews, presents an important insight for anyone concerned about real change, anyone who passionately desires a new vision of the world. While the utopian longing usually begins with our institutions, true change is always based on our personal connections with others. A better society, while influenced by benevolent regulation and governmental progress, depends on developing trusting relationships between individual people. When people settle into trusting relationships, they are open to vision, to dreaming together to change larger systems. In trusting, enthusiastic relationships, new models are born because people are open to larger understandings. Even more than thinking up great schemes for change, such people simply become open to new ways of being together, the fundamental substance of a true utopia.

A whole lifetime is short.
I cannot depend on anything that passes away.
— St. Teresa of Avila

Impermanence warns us not to put our trust in this life, but to look beyond to its source in the Divine. This is precisely what St. Teresa of Avila did. As the Buddha did with his teaching on impermanence, Teresa looked to the stability of eternal reality, which she came to realize in the intimacy of mystical union. How could she trade that absolute reality for the passing joys of this world? If we want ultimate happiness that does not dissipate with time, we must learn the ways of the spiritual life. At the same time, we need balance. We cannot reject what is good in this life, even though life's brevity means nothing lasts. Let us also "store up our treasures in Heaven."

[259]

If anybody asks what Sufism is, what kind of religion it is,
the answer is that Sufism is the religion of the heart,
the religion in which the thing of primary importance
is to seek God in the heart of humankind.

— Hazrat Inayat Khan

⁓

Hazrat Inayat Khan, father of Pir Valayat Khan and founder of the Sufi Order of the West, was also a brilliant writer and spiritual master. Sufism is the heart of Islam, the enlightened understanding and practice that grows in one who discovers the Divine experientially by turning within. Sufism is the surrender to the way of Divine Love. This surrender to Allah's love is the key to the Qur'an, at least for those who are awakened to the mystical life in Islam. The Sufi always seeks the path of peace because that is what love does and requires. Sufi mystics are sensitive to the Divine Presence in our deepest being in the heart, in our capacity for selfless love, a love that is derived from Allah and is Allah.

[260]

We must create a society in which a person does not have to betray inner sensitivity, inner essence.

— Vimala Thakar

〜

Vimala Thakar, an Indian social and political activist in the spirit of Gandhi and author of *The Eloquence of Living,* challenges us to enlarge our vision of society to encompass an authentic vision of our true selves. Often our present society tramples on sensitivity. Our inclinations toward love and mercy are compromised by the competition and materialism that rule our world. Our society forces us to betray our nature in order to conform and get ahead. In truth, our inner sensitivity is grounded in a caring heart, or the good heart, as the Tibetans say. All of us share this deeper nature, which becomes obscured by the demands of our fast-paced, anonymous, indifferent culture. As much as we can, we have to be true to ourselves, even without the cooperation of social systems. This inner essence is our gift to one another. It is part of the Divine's presence in us.

The soul that walks in love
neither rests nor grows tired.

— St. John of the Cross

As with all the saints, no matter what tradition we choose, John of the Cross demonstrated in his life the inexhaustible nature of Divine Love. The same love that inspired the great sixteenth-century Spanish mystic, and all sages in every age and region of the planet, also inspired Mother Teresa, St. Francis of Assisi, and Mahatma Gandhi. The person who knows and is sustained by this love never grows weary of its endless demands. Do you walk in the light of this extraordinary love or is your love more particular and discriminating? Learn to open your being to the greater love witnessed in the example of the saints and watch your capacity expand, your compassion grow, and your generosity deepen.

Happiness lies not in feeding and fueling our attachments,
but in reducing and relinquishing them.

— Roger Walsh

Roger Walsh, an Australian-born psychotherapist, professor of psychiatry at the University of California at Irvine and author of *Essential Spirituality*, pinpoints a very basic principle of the spiritual journey. The Buddha, Jesus, Shankara, the prophets of the biblical tradition, mystic seers everywhere and in all times have all emphasized that we only enjoy lasting happiness when we free ourselves of desires. They are almost always fixations on impermanent things: possessions, influence, fame, or sex. Until we attain *inner* freedom by letting go of our attachments, we are not really free, nor can we be truly, meaningfully happy. When we attain the objects of our desires, the satisfaction we realize is hollow and our desires graduate to the next object. Genuine happiness transcends desire, as we attain abiding rest in the Divine.

The highest degree of the highest virtue is detachment.
— Meister Eckhart

Following Roger Walsh's wise observation, Meister Eckhart's teaching demonstrates that mysticism truly crosses traditions and philosophies. What might seem distinctly Buddhist at first hearing are actually the words of Eckhart, a thirteenth-century Christian. Detachment is a very practical psychological skill; it cuts away at the emotional baggage that slows us down, the turmoil of the emotional center associated with our desires and attachments, what Buddhism calls "afflictive emotions." Detachment doesn't mean indifference toward others. It means that we can truly love others but in a nonpossessive way. Possessiveness of those we love is one of the worst forms of attachment. Detachment doesn't mean that we love less, but that we love with real maturity, depth, and ultimacy — desiring true happiness for those we love, placing their well-being before our own preferences.

How is heaven attained?
The attainment of heaven is freedom from cravings.
— Shankara

⌒

Again we see how the notion of detachment crosses borders. Ninth-century Hindu teacher Shankara — or as he is called in India, Shankaracharya, meaning Shankara the great spiritual teacher — is the untiring advocate of *advaita,* or nonduality, the mystical school that proclaims the Brahman, the Godhead, to be the substance of all reality. Like the Buddha's Third Noble Truth, which instructs that extinction of craving is the way to liberation from suffering, Shankara's guidance here is meant to bring us to the same state of inner freedom, equanimity, peace, and presence to others. Discipline of our desires, especially our powerful longings, is the way to advance to the ultimate level of awareness, which is Heaven. To attain this essential inner freedom is a difficult struggle because we are such creatures of habit. What is required is utter determination.

[265]

When the last leaf falls, when the last drop of water
dies out, when the ozone layer is already destroyed,
will it be too late to understand
that money is not going to save us?

— Tove

Anne Rowthorn, a passionate environmental activist and editor of *Earth and All the Stars*, includes in her anthology this poem from a Swedish child named Tove, which she took from a collection called *Children's State of the World Handbook*. With the clear-eyed wisdom that comes from those who haven't yet been clouded by the preoccupation with money, Tove has comprehended the fundamental question that people who run the corporate world have not or will not address. It is short-sighted economic policies that have brought us to the grave situation we now find ourselves in. Unless corporate leaders experience a sudden epiphany, or the governments of the world drastically limit their harm, the future of humanity is in serious doubt. The earth will survive without us. The question is really our own survival. Our approach to this ecological crisis is the primary moral and spiritual issue of our age.

Half the people in the world think that the
metaphors of their religious traditions . . . are facts.
And the other half contends that they are not facts at
all. As a result we have people who consider themselves
believers because they accept metaphors as facts,
and we have others who classify themselves as atheists
because they think religious metaphors are lies.

— Joseph Campbell

As we can see in this quote from *Thou Art That*, the mythologist Joseph Campbell understood that many of people's arguments over religion, particularly Christian religion, stem from interpretation of religious scripture. The powerful metaphors meant to describe moral and mystical experience are often interpreted literally, both by atheists and fundamentalists. Interpretation is always up to the individual, but taking the beautiful language of scripture to reveal Christ's mystical experience metaphorically gives us greater personal insight into the spiritual journey.

[267]

*The faces of those who move towards the Heaven of
truth and bliss acquire a wonderful shining spiritual
beauty.... All attain to the gladsome springtime
of youth, with a beauty surpassing anything
the mortal mind can conceive.*

— Emanuel Swedenborg

Emanuel Swedenborg (1688–1772) was a Swedish
philosopher who wrote about religious notions of
Heaven in his *Heaven and its Wonders*. Beauty is an
attribute of the Divine that we human beings are given
to share in, but it is never ours by right or by ownership. God is total beauty itself. Heaven is complete
beatitude, the greatest beatitude, the eternal happiness
of complete communion with God. The happiness of
the beatific state — the heavenly realm's glory, tranquility, harmony, and emanating love — cannot be conceived by our minds in our present state of existence.

[268]

*You always carry within yourself the very thing that
you need for the fulfillment of your life purpose.*

— Malidoma Somé

~

African writer Malidoma Somé, who wrote *Of Water
and the Spirit,* presents the wisdom that the key to our
ultimate fulfillment is not outside of us, waiting to be
searched for and found. It is within each of us. In fact,
one of the greatest fruits of spiritual life is a deep,
mature, effective, and accurate self-knowledge. Each
person has a mission, a work they must contribute to
the whole. It appears vaguely at first, a nagging dissat-
isfaction or an inkling of desire for greater things, but
within a disciplined inner journey, the process of becoming honest with ourselves, we can come to realize
our life purpose. To fulfill this task, we need to touch
the inner fire that propels us forward, the passion to do
good, to serve both the Divine and the human family.
We know in the depths of our being that our nature
holds our sacred purpose. We only need to be true to
it, to pursue it without fail.

As long as the Earth can make a spring every year,
I can. As long as the Earth can flower and produce
nurturing fruit, I can, because I'm the Earth.
I won't give up until the Earth gives up.

— Alice Walker

The wonderful writer Alice Walker, winner of the Pulitzer Prize for her novel *The Color Purple*, gives expression to the determination, perseverance, and hope that come from an invincible faith in the immutability of nature. Walker writes of being able to muster hope and renewal by taking inspiration from the cycle of the seasons. Each one of us can bring forth a spring in our own lives, and we can be as fruitful in our own way. We are each the Earth from the perspective of our own life and its purpose, its contribution to all sentient beings and the Earth itself. It is this kind of determination and commitment we need to survive, to thrive, to bring justice to the world, transform consciousness, and advance in our own lives. This courage has the power to overcome the fear, anxiety, and pessimism that may plague us. Are you ready to bring forth spring in your life, and are you prepared to blossom and bear fruit for others? If you doubt, look within for that place of strength and determination.

Whence come I and whither go I? That is the great
unfathomable question, the same for every one of us.
Science has no answer to it.

— Erwin Schrödinger

Erwin Schrödinger (1887–1961) was awarded the
Nobel Prize in physics in 1933 for his pioneering work
on waves, culminating in "Schrödinger's wave equa-
tion." Like Albert Einstein, he clearly grasped the limitations of the scientific method. Of course science can
describe in beautiful, intricate detail the *how* of the
world, the cosmos, and life, but it can offer nothing
about the *why*. All of science, like all of experience, happens within the matrix of consciousness, a focus of
study that ultimately stymies scientific inquiry. Where
we came from and why, as well as our purpose here,
are questions that can only be truly understood in the
course of the spiritual life.

Though words are spoken to explain the Void,
the Void as such can never be expressed.

— Tilopa

These words by Tilopa (989–1069), a Tibetan Buddhist Tantric master, appear in his poem "The Song of Mahamudra." Tilopa was the first Mahamudra master of *shunyata,* or emptiness as the basis of existence. In Sanskrit, *shunyata* has an elusive meaning. Some call it the "silence from which everything emanates," yet it means "openness." But the most common meaning is the Void, the essential emptiness of reality because of its impermanence. This conditioned, relative existence is empty of intrinsic reality and so is void of being in any absolute sense. The Void as a metaphysical absolute, or the Unconditioned Reality, is another story altogether, and here, as Tilopa tells us, words fail to express its truth. The Void is ineffable; its reality cannot be captured in words or concepts, since it is a transcendent, infinite reality.

They are all fire, and no light; all husk, and no kernel.

— Rumi

⌒

Rumi's poetic metaphor takes on profound meaning when we learn that he was writing about the Islamic extremists of his time — the thirteenth century. Clearly, nothing has changed. But fundamentalism and extremism exist in all religions. No matter the tradition, extremism and fanaticism tear people away from the Divine, away from true enlightenment; they distract from love, compassion, and kindness. The authentic spiritual life is about the inner light and the kernel, not the external fire or violent passion, which typically take their fuel from hate. These preoccupations are about the husk, the surface level of religion. The *jihad* is not out there in the world, but in one's own heart. It is the inner struggle with one's own attachments, vices, ignorance, and fears.

We cannot do great things,
only little things with great love.

— Mother Teresa

Doing "little things with great love" defined Mother Teresa's life and witness in the world. She knew that great opportunities are rare and that the little opportunities that come our way every day provide the occasions for us to grow in love by transcending ourselves. It takes considerable awareness from moment to moment to recognize these little opportunities. We need to be alert to the invitations we receive in each moment. We can respond with love in all the situations of life and practice compassion without counting the cost. And of course a spiritual practice of meditation or prayer can help prepare us to do everything with extraordinary love in each moment. One of the reasons we are here in this existence is to learn and hone this skill of great love. The great achievements our society celebrates often have no beneficial effect on anyone. It is really the little things that are important.

At the end of life we will be judged
on how much we have loved.

— St. John of the Cross

⌒

God is love itself. Therefore, it is only fitting that our lives here and afterward are also about love — that we are here to perfect this Divine Love in everything we do, say, think, and feel. This quality of love is not sentimental nor discriminatory, nor is it limited in its range; it is freely given, responding to the needs that present themselves in the sufferings of others. We are always faced with the same choice: ourselves or others. It is easy to ignore the needs of others. We can walk past homeless people in our cities, pretending we don't see them. We can argue over petty disagreements with our spouses or curse the drivers who slight us. It's always easier to dismiss our responsibility toward others by focusing on our own matters. But we do not fool God, ourselves, or others. When the call comes, will you be ready to look at your life and examine how you responded to love?

Absorbed in the Self, the sage is freed from identity
with the body and lives in blissful consciousness.
The Self is the immortal, the fearless;
the Self is Brahman. This Brahman is eternal truth.

— Chandogya Upanishad

In this passage, the Chandogya Upanishad is identifying the inner reality of the mystical life as *atmavidya* and *brahmavidya,* the experiential awareness of the Divine Presence. The enlightened person is liberated from identifying with his or her body, which is part of the conditioned, impermanent state called life. The Hindu view is very clear that we are not our bodies, since they pass away, nor are we our emotions, for the same reason. Nor are we our minds, for they are equally conditioned by this relative existence. Beyond the body, the emotional being, our imaginative faculty, our mind and thoughts, is our immortal self, the Divine Presence in us at the basis of our very being. One with the self, the Atman is in blissful awareness and is not bothered by the body and the passing states of this world. This text calls us back to our home in the Divine Consciousness, our ultimate actual identity.

Emptiness is the ground of everything.
Thanks to emptiness, everything is possible.

— Thich Nhat Hanh

~

Vietnamese Zen monk Thich Nhat Hanh makes this seemingly enigmatic remark in his book *The Heart of Understanding: Commentaries on the Prajnaparamita Heart Sutra,* which explores one of the most important of the sacred works of the Buddhist Dharma, or teachings. Emptiness, *shunyata,* is an absolute in Buddhist metaphysics and mysticism. The great Buddhist text *The Heart Sutra* follows the constant back and forth between emptiness and form. All form comes out of emptiness, and all emptiness is filled with form. Emptiness is analogous to the Godhead, especially in its transcendent state, and in that state all potential exists and comes to be in the realm of manifestation. But all form is impermanent; it returns to the primordial nature, the transcendent mystery beyond this life and this world. Form cannot be seen except in relationship to emptiness. Emptiness is the matrix of being, and everything that is, can be, or will be is present in the emptiness.

Think about yourself:
your temple of God, the body;
your spirit of God, the soul;
the flow of God, the mind.

— Yogi Bhajan

⌒

This wise saying of Yogi Bhajan, a great promoter of Kundalini Yoga, appears on a tea bag of his Yogi Tea. With every tea bag comes an adage or teaching to nourish the spirit. Here, the yogi wants us to keep in mind that our bodies, souls, and minds are extensions of the Divine, that God acts through us by accessing these elements of our beings and many others. The Hindu notion of the body's role in relation to God has a parallel in the Christian view that the body is the temple of the Holy Spirit. What Yogi Bhajan is saying is that our bodies, minds, and souls must be consecrated to God and the Divine Purpose because that is why we are here. The body, soul, and mind must work together in this purpose through each one of us. If we are in harmony with the Divine Purpose, God's temple, spirit, and flow in our lives are similarly in harmony.

I desire, Brother Wolf, to make peace between you and [the people], so that you may offend no more, and they shall forgive you your past offenses.

— St. Francis of Assisi

⌒

In *Fioretti,* or *The Little Flowers of St. Francis of Assisi,* a wonderful book of stories from St. Francis's life, the saint seeks to make peace with a wolf who had been terrorizing the town of Gubbio, stealing chickens, frightening people, and disturbing the peace. Francis created peace between the wolf and the townsfolk with an agreement that they would look after all the needs of the wolf and the wolf would behave himself. Soon the wolf became a beloved pet of Gubbio, known for his love, affection, and protection. He came in time to be called the Holy Wolf of Gubbio. This is an example of the saint's power over animals, but it also speaks to the workings of grace and love in all of us. We have the same power as St. Francis to transform animosity into love. Are you open to this power of grace and love that extends to all sentient beings?

*A Jew cannot meet God; nor can a Christian, Muslim,
Hindu, Buddhist, Confucian, or Taoist. No labeled person
can meet the Unlabeled and the Unlabelable. Each religious
tradition must be self-transcending. Each must lead its
students to a point of departure and help them make
the leap from tradition to Truth, God, the nondual
Reality that is the Source and Substance of all things.*

— Rami Shapiro

Rami Shapiro, a rabbi, interfaith leader, writer, and
author of *Minyan: The Ten Principles for Living a Life of
Integrity,* concentrates our minds and hearts on the
sober realization that finding God mystically requires
us to transcend the words or doctrines of any tradition
we follow. The word *minyan* in rabbinic understanding
refers to forming a quorum, which requires ten Jewish
men. Rami Shapiro takes this notion and creates a
vision of Jewish spiritual life on a daily basis with ten
principles he unfolds. They all lead to the overpowering, existential conviction of finding the Godhead beyond the confines of tradition. For Shapiro, it is only
when we know God directly in the mystical way that
we really know God at all.

A contemplative act is done for its own sake.

— Raimon Panikkar

Raimon Panikkar, a brilliant cross-cultural thinker and writer, reveals a fundamental truth about the nature of contemplation that should be remembered in the current commercialization of spirituality. We tend to think about the practical results of an action. We typically do something to accomplish an end, like cutting down a forest to build a subdivision, attending school to get a job, selling a product to make money. But contemplation has no practical goal. It's an end in itself. Contemplation, opening to the Divine in the depths of one's own heart, mind, or consciousness, is about *being* rather than *doing*. We say, "Don't just stand there, do something!" The *doing* of the contemplative act is its *being*, much like a flower. A flower is simply immersed in being, in the act of presence, of opening itself to the light and warmth of the sun, wind, rain, and soil. In the same way, learning from the flowers and trees, we can just *be*, in contemplation.

*This much is certain, that once we make up our minds
to seek God, he is already seeking us
much more eagerly, and he is not going
to let anything happen to prevent his purpose.*

— Thomas Keating

Understanding the true reciprocity of the mystical life lends us considerable strength. Thomas Keating, speaking from long experience, emphasizes the fact that God wills for us to seek him, and that is actually our purpose for being: to search for a relationship with him and to find him in the intimacy of union and a communion of love. Abbot Thomas points out that when we commit ourselves to God, his commitment to us is far greater than ours to him. Long before we made the decision to seek the Divine, the Divine was wholeheartedly seeking us, like the Hound of Heaven in the Francis Thompson poem of the same name. His purpose is relentless. This mystical relationship is why we are here, why we were born. Our existence is a summons to this eternal gift that we could never merit. The spiritual life is a creative balance between effort and grace: our effort and God's grace. It is the treasure of God's generosity.

Closer is He than breathing
and nearer than hands and feet.
— Alfred Lord Tennyson

The Qur'an tells us that Allah is nearer to us than our jugular vein. St. Augustine declares to God that our hearts were made for him and that he is more intimate to each one of us than we are to ourselves. The English poet Alfred Lord Tennyson beautifully describes how God is more intimate to us than our own hearts. This proximity can be explained in realizing that everything happens within the Divine Consciousness. It can equally be said that God is within us, dwells in the depths of our being or heart. What we discern here is a mutual in-dwelling: we in God, and God in us. Recognizing this proximity is what the spiritual life is all about.

[283]

The last will be first, and the first, last.

— Gospel of Matthew

This passage in Matthew's Gospel (20:16) alerts us that the way of Christ is the reverse of the way of the world. It appears in the parable of the workers in the vineyard — the ones who come at the last hour receive the same wage as those who came at the first hour — but it has an application beyond the logic of the parable itself. In the Kingdom of Heaven, the first are those who were last in this world, those who chose the path of humility, love, and compassion. Many of the least in this life, those ignored by passersby, will have a high place in God's Kingdom. Those who have everything they want in this life, who are among the first here and who don't see the plight of the last, will be last in the Kingdom of Heaven.

[284]

If one observes the Way of Heaven,
and maintains Its doings [as his own],
all that he has to do is accomplished.

— Taoist aphorism

The Taoist work *The Classic of the Harmony of the Seen and the Unseen* stresses the celebrated theme of the Taoist mystics and philosophers: harmony with the order of Tao. As is typical in Taoist philosophy, this statement de-emphasizes the value of traditional accomplishment yet guarantees a different kind of success and happiness if one lives in and from the Tao, the Divine Reality. Observing in our lives, inner attitudes, and actions the nature of the Way and accepting it as part of ourselves is living in harmony with nature and the Divine. If the work we do is the work of the Tao, the Way of nature and the cosmos, then what we have to do in life will be "accomplished," springing forth from this deepest commitment.

The very fact that you desire to be enlightened
will give you the power to be enlightened.
That is the fuel. Flame it. Fuel it.

— Marsha Sinetar

St. Augustine says that the desire for God means that
you have already found God. Desire opens the door to
greater awareness and insight. Marsha Sinetar, author
of *Do What You Love: The Money Will Follow*, stresses the
purity of desire, the ready willingness to be enlightened.
Desire, the intensity of our commitment to enlightenment or salvation, empowers us to achieve it. It is what
propels us forward, what sparks and consistently energizes the search for enlightenment or salvation. Yet as
we are reminded by the Taoist philosophies of the previous quotation or the Hindu philosophies that inspire
the teachings of Dr. Chopra in the next quotation,
enlightenment cannot be forced. Through hard work,
effort, and desire, enlightenment comes in its own time.

If you want anything in the physical universe,
you have to relinquish your attachment to the outcome.

— Deepak Chopra, M.D.

This insight, inspired by the subtle teaching of the Bhagavad Gita, is related to the path of karma yoga, the way of selfless service. When we're unattached to the results of our work and undertake labor for the sake of others or the welfare of the community, we attain our goals. If we really desire something in this physical realm, we must let go of the eventual result or exactly how our desires manifest in the lives of others. We cannot control the outcome; we will get what we want, the Hindu tradition tells us, but often with unforeseen results. We must abandon any attachment to these results and trust in the process. Practicing detachment leads us to happiness and success.

Sacred partnership is a rich and deep friendship
between equals that brings us sanctuary,
soul growth, and sizzle.

— Sue Patton Thoele

Author of *The Woman's Book of Courage,* Sue Patton
Thoele presents the ideal of mature relationship. Like the
writings of Riane Eisler, who promotes partnership over
the domination that has overtaken our society, Thoele
describes a relationship predicated upon mutual awareness, respect, equality, and a highly developed love that
has progressed beyond mere sentiment and attachment.
It reminds me of the poet R.M. Rilke's description of the
ideal marriage, in which two people guard one another's
solitude. She names such a relationship sacred because it
involves the spiritual life of two people who live and grow
together in the dimension of their inner lives, their souls.
We can also extend this model to our business and professional relationships, recognizing the possibility for
each transaction to be of mutual benefit and respect. The
relationship of sacred partnerships forms a sanctuary
that fosters both the inner growth of individuals and
outer societal growth when applied in that direction. It is
powerful and a real treasure.

Play keeps us vital and alive.
It gives us an enthusiasm for life that is irreplaceable.
Without it, life just doesn't taste good.

— Lucia Capacchione

A wonderful international organization in Chicago called Play for Peace uses the value of play in bringing conflicting communities together. No matter how hard we work along the spiritual path, without a joyful, exuberant sense of play and humor, we'll get nowhere. Too often those pursuing the spiritual life, in their dogged quest for Divine Consciousness, get caught up in humorless singularity of mind. Lucia Capacchione, author of *Putting Your Talent to Work,* emphasizes here the importance of play in our lives. Play gives our relationships color and taste, fascination and creativity. It shows us how alive we can be. In its deepest sense, play is a contemplative act. We lose our nagging sense of self, our endless loops of preoccupation, and become lost in the present. Play has no end beyond itself, though it gives us so many benefits.

Meditation ... could be defined as the art
of modulating consciousness.

— Pir Valayat Khan

The Sufi is a mystic who is constantly remembering God, or Allah, as illustrated by the great Sufi master Pir Valayat Khan. The "art of modulating consciousness," meditation is a process of gradually becoming more and more attuned to the Divine Reality, the activity of remembering God. Gradually, as we learn to fine-tune our normally uncontrolled thoughts and preoccupations, we tune to the Divinity already ever-present in our consciousness. To modulate our consciousness through meditation is to allow for its transformation, the change from self-preoccupation to God-realization, from ego-fixation to Divine Love. Meditation is a way into union with God. It is also the path of becoming like the Divine. In becoming more and more like the Divine, the person following this path increases his capacity to love others. Meditation will change your life.

Blessed are the merciful, for they shall obtain mercy.

— Gospel of Matthew

In a beautifully interspiritual teaching, again from the beatitudes (Matthew 5:7), Jesus teaches a Christian expression of the karmic principle. If we are merciful to others, Jesus says, we are blessed, both because we have the character and the wisdom to be merciful and because we will receive mercy ourselves. Although the gifts are many, the enlightened ones take the path of mercy not because of the rewards but because they are united to God in his Holy Spirit. Because they love God, they seek to be like him, to love as he loves, to be as he is, and to respond to the sufferings of others.

What happens after death is so unspeakably glorious
that our imagination and feelings do not suffice
to form an even approximate conception of it.

— Carl Jung

Although Sigmund Freud was fascinated with a mystical state he called the "oceanic sense," he was mostly an atheist. In contrast, Carl Jung was an eclectic and wide-ranging mystic. The above observation appeared in his memoirs, *Memories, Dreams, Reflections*. Jung had a powerful intuition of the Heavenly Reality after death. He emphasizes the essentially ineffable character of Paradise and the joys of this eternal realm. More than a place, Heaven is God; it is living forever in the Divine Consciousness. None of us can conceive the glorious reality of being with God forever. In mystical union with the Source, we have an intuition and some experience of Heaven. We feel that it's about the fullness of happiness in the total actuality of love. But in truth it is beyond the experience and conception of this life.

The first love affair we need to consummate successfully is with ourselves, because only then will we be ready for relationships with others.

— Nathaniel Branden

While it may seem obvious and border on a cliché, we cannot remind ourselves too often that a healthy and loving sense of ourselves must come before we can love others. Nathaniel Branden, author of *The Art of Living Consciously,* helps us to remember that success in any relationship stems from a successful primary relationship with ourselves. Loving ourselves is not self-centeredness, but rather healthy appreciation and self-esteem. Nor is self-love narcissistic. It is a regarding of oneself with honesty and most of all a sense of compassion. If we have this healthy relationship with ourselves, then we are ready to pursue relationships with others.

We cannot put off living until we are ready.
The most salient characteristic of life is its urgency,
"here and now" without any possible postponement.
Life is fired at us point-blank.

— José Ortega y Gasset

Human nature constantly suppresses a healthy under-standing of our mortality. Without conscious effort or constant reminders, we fall back into the illusion that life will go on forever, that we always have the chance to begin again. The Spanish existentialist philosopher José Ortega y Gasset identifies the urgency that faces us all. All we have is the here and now whether we like it or not, yet it is so easy not to live our lives in the here and now. Life can pass us by if we live either in the future, focusing on expectations, projections, and wishes for ourselves, families, and friends, or in the past through our memories and regrets of what has been. Conditions will never be just right. Life begins when we decide to begin. We have to decide in each moment to accept the challenge of being and just live to the fullest in each moment, with the happy recognition of life's urgency.

Chaos is infinitely complex order.

— David Bohm

⌒

David Bohm, visionary physicist and author of the groundbreaking book *Wholeness and the Implicate Order,* made this extraordinary observation in an interview with Michael Toms on *New Dimensions Radio.* Chaos may truly be an incredibly subtle order, so infinitely complex that physics and mathematics cannot fully describe its laws. Like the ungraspable nature of the Divine, the order of chaos flits in and out of our ability to comprehend it. Applying this rich insight to human life, the question arises: Do you discern the Divine Order in life's chaos? What does it mean to you?

Affection . . . is the humblest love. It gives itself no airs.
People can be proud of being "in love," or of friendship.
Affection is modest — even furtive and shame-faced.

— C. S. Lewis

Often sitting in the shadow of the more celebrated romantic love, with its violent passions and uncontrollable urges, this subtle form of love is heartfelt and gives itself often without thought of return. Based on simple appreciation, it has a modesty of expectation that doesn't approach the commitments of a spousal relationship or a very deep, spiritual kind of friendship, but it is no less real in its demands on the heart and the will. Affection is simple, direct, almost contemplative in its expression, since it has no goal beyond being loving toward another.

Do you see O my brothers and sisters?
It is not chaos or death — it is form, union, plan —
it is eternal life — it is Happiness.

— Walt Whitman

The great American poet Walt Whitman viewed this existence through his poetic and mystical intuition. Here he speaks with poetic authority about the direction toward which we are all moving: eternal life. He understood that dark notions about death were misunderstandings of why we are here. What we find here is evidence of a cosmic plan, which leads to union with the Divine. We are destined for this high estate of eternal happiness. It takes wisdom, divine illumination, to give us direction to our home. If we can become inwardly attuned to the Divine Presence within, we will understand our nature and our ultimate belonging to God.

If we take eternity to mean
not infinite temporal duration, but timelessness,
eternal life is theirs who live in the present.

— Ludwig Wittgenstein

This extraordinary philosopher deconstructs a common but partial conception of eternity. While we often think of eternity as infinite time, it also means timelessness, found only in the present or the now. Wittgenstein's mystical life led him ultimately to leave academic philosophy, an arena in which he was a star. He echoed what contemporary spiritual teacher and philosopher Eckhart Tolle has emphasized: The present is the entry point into the Eternal Now, and this now is the beginning of realizing the Everlasting Now, which people understand by the designation "eternity." The more we enter into this now, the more we experience its timeless or eternal properties: wisdom, understanding, compassion, kindness, mercy, sensitivity, integration, and joy.

My experience is that most people who think they
are beyond the intellect actually haven't quite
gotten up to it yet.

— Ken Wilber

When the profound integral philosopher Ken Wilber
makes this observation, he has in mind, perhaps, the
medieval philosophical understanding of the intellect.
The word *intellect* in English derives from the Latin
word *intellectus*, which connotes having understood. It
is deeper, more comprehensive, and more subtle than
reason; it is akin to the operations of wisdom rather
than the mere workings of the rational mind. May we
all aspire to and reach this deep understanding.

The journey to God is merely the reawakening
of the knowledge of where you are always,
and what you are forever. It is a journey
without distance to a goal that has never changed.

— *A Course in Miracles*

Our journey to God is actually a journey of self-discovery in the Divine. Plato, Plotinus, Origen, St. Thomas Aquinas, and Indian philosophers — all of these historical figures had a similar vision as the one stated here in *A Course in Miracles,* a book of channeled spiritual wisdom. According to *A Course in Miracles,* we have always been in God; we came from the Divine, and this is our destiny and our home forever. The spiritual journey is not to a place, but to the ultimate reality of Divine Consciousness. There is thus no distance involved in the inner sojourn. The spiritual journey is a process that reveals the end, the destination, the goal that is essentially changeless: union with God. And each one of us is a member of the Divine Family.

Intuition is the ability as Spirit to know what is unavailable to the body and its senses. It is the ability to have access to all information or Wisdom that ever existed or will exist.

— Helen Vandeman

We often dismiss our intuitive knowing, or at least demean it, by thinking less of it than we do more conventional, direct forms of learning. Helen Vandeman, author of *We Are One: Using Intuition to Awaken to Truth*, gives us an expansive view of intuition, a capacity we all share once we become receptive to it. Intuitive ability doesn't require reason, sense, or experience to function. It reaches out spontaneously and just knows. Yet it is subtle. We all experience it, but not everyone has learned to recognize it or trust its reliability, truth, and insight. Helen Vandeman has devoted her life to teaching others how to develop and use their intuition. To honor it we simply have to listen to it, that subtle voice underneath the noise of our thinking and reasoning. If we do embrace it as part of ourselves, it will lead us into the ways of the Divine and guide us along every step.

Time's not an object but an idea.
It will be extinguished in the mind.

— Fyodor Dostoyevsky

Fyodor Dostoyevsky, the celebrated Russian writer, expresses here that time is a subjective reality, rather than an objective certitude. Time is a conception of the mind and can be overcome in the mind. The passing of time is something we all experience in our own consciousness, in our own inner subjective perception. Perhaps it has no real objective reality as we commonly understand objectivity. It would not be true to say, however, that time is an illusion, a mere concoction of the mind for the practical necessity of understanding the world, life, and reality. Time is a reality that requires consciousness to be, because it is only within consciousness that it is known.

[302]

One instant is eternity;
eternity is in the now;
When you see through this one instant,
you see through the one who sees.

— Wu-Men

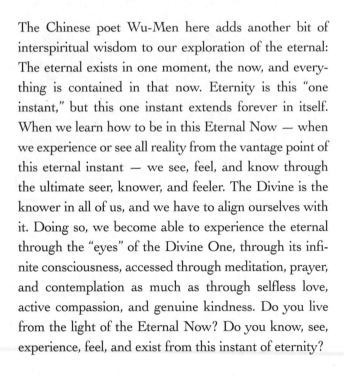

The Chinese poet Wu-Men here adds another bit of interspiritual wisdom to our exploration of the eternal: The eternal exists in one moment, the now, and everything is contained in that now. Eternity is this "one instant," but this one instant extends forever in itself. When we learn how to be in this Eternal Now — when we experience or see all reality from the vantage point of this eternal instant — we see, feel, and know through the ultimate seer, knower, and feeler. The Divine is the knower in all of us, and we have to align ourselves with it. Doing so, we become able to experience the eternal through the "eyes" of the Divine One, through its infinite consciousness, accessed through meditation, prayer, and contemplation as much as through selfless love, active compassion, and genuine kindness. Do you live from the light of the Eternal Now? Do you know, see, experience, feel, and exist from this instant of eternity?

[303]

People see God every day;
they just don't recognize him.

— Pearl Bailey

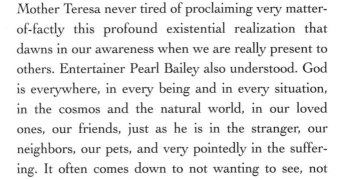

Mother Teresa never tired of proclaiming very matter-of-factly this profound existential realization that dawns in our awareness when we are really present to others. Entertainer Pearl Bailey also understood. God is everywhere, in every being and in every situation, in the cosmos and the natural world, in our loved ones, our friends, just as he is in the stranger, our neighbors, our pets, and very pointedly in the suffering. It often comes down to not wanting to see, not wanting to turn ourselves toward suffering, thinking that we will only see pain and darkness. It may seem difficult, but once we make the effort we realize that we will not be pulled toward the dark if we recognize the profound suffering in others, but rather toward the light.

[304]

Failure is the key to success;
each mistake teaches us something.

— Morihei Ueshiba

It's always easier to sit back on the sidelines and point
out the failings of others as they strive toward achieving something. It's much harder to try and fail ourselves. But as Morihei Ueshiba, the founder of the
martial art aikido and author of *The Art of Peace,* shows
here, failure is not an end but a beginning, because it
reveals something that will assist us in moving forward.
Ueshiba should know. I used to practice aikido and
was constantly failing! Of course we don't typically
view failure as a key to success because it is painful.
But we all experience failure in our lives. It's part of
growth and maturity. What we learn from each
instance of failure becomes the basis of our ultimate
success if we approach each mistake with awareness
and learn to make the necessary changes. Do not flee
the moments of failure.

The will of God is manifest in each moment,
an immense ocean which the heart only fathoms
in so far as it overflows with faith, trust and love.

— Jean Pierre de Caussade

Although we typically think of present moment awareness as a Buddhist principle, Jean Pierre de Caussade
(1675–1751), a French Jesuit and author of the classic
Abandonment to Divine Providence, understood well the
importance of mindfulness to the present moment. He
realized from his own direct mystical inner experience
and his awareness of life that the Divine will reveal
itself from moment to moment. What God requires of
us in each moment is our surrender to him, the deepening of our love for him and his will, and our compassionate, loving response to all others. But there is much
more! God's will is not static; it is pure immensity, an
ocean of unlimited possibilities. God's will embraces
the totality of our development and faith. Trust and
love are the keys that open us to the fullness of God's
will for us.

The true heaven is everywhere, even in that very place
where you stand and walk.... If man's eyes were
opened, he would see God everywhere in this heaven,
for heaven stands in the innermost moving everywhere.

— Jacob Boehme

Jacob Boehme (1575–1624), a German Protestant mystic and shoemaker, makes a claim for experiencing Heaven, or the Divine, in every step we take. In order to be aware of and sensitive to the presence of Heaven, we have to, as he says, open our eyes. The primary experience of Heaven, however, is within us, in that "innermost" center of ourselves that then moves in all directions, everywhere. But to see Heaven in this life, we have to be made aware through an unfolding sensitivity that develops through prayer, meditation, and contemplation. This is how our eyes are opened.

Only connect.
Wherever you are, right now,
pay attention. Forever.

— Sylvia Boorstein

Mindfulness is the continuous act of being aware in the present moment, of paying attention by extending a meditative state beyond the sitting cushion into all the activities of our lives. But, as Buddhist teacher Sylvia Boorstein, author of *It's Easier Than You Think* and *Don't Just Do Something, Sit There,* says here, we pay attention so that we may fulfill the further teaching, the goal in each moment of connecting with others, of recognizing in each moment the opportunity and invitation to be present to others. In this realization, Sylvia Boorstein's understanding parallels that of the great Jewish philosopher Martin Buber, who views each moment in life as essentially a meeting with others, or *the* other, a meeting in which we can connect with them as a thou, affirming their dignity as persons in the image and likeness of the Divine. Although coming from different traditions, the quality of awareness is the same. The work of life is to "only connect."

*Paradoxically, it's most often our smallest,
most anonymously done good works that have
the greatest spiritual impact in and on this world.*

— Thom Hartmann

Thom Hartmann, an eloquent writer and radio talk
show host of the nationally syndicated *Thom Hartmann
Show*, echoes Mother Teresa's teachings that little acts
of love are most important in life. These small good
works have results we do not foresee; their spiritual
effects in the world are often unknown to us, but they
are real. We human beings tend to think in terms of
great, public works of goodness, but Hartmann calls us
to consider the sanctity of the small, hidden acts of
love, compassion, and kindness that are the response
of a heart open to goodness. Incidentally, Hartmann
not only talks about such acts, he performs them. Once
on a ten-hour bus ride to New Delhi, India, returning
from a conference with the Dalai Lama in Dharmsala,
Thom, formerly a massage therapist, gave out skilled
massages to anyone who wanted one!

*If you are really determined
to be on the good side of life,
the forces of the universe are there to help you.*

— Robert Muller

⌐∽

If we align ourselves with goodness, the universe — the Divine, Infinite Awareness, the Absolute — will direct and assist us at every juncture. Robert Muller, former Assistant Secretary General of the United Nations and author of numerous books, including *Most of All They Taught Me Happiness*, learned from his experience as a world leader that cultivating a good heart and a life of compassion, love, and kindness makes the Divine, "the forces of the universe," available to us. Those that give themselves to the service of the higher purpose find the way open to them. If you strive to do great things, the universe will support you.

As a person leaves an old garment and puts on one
that is new, the Spirit leaves the mortal body and
wanders on to one that is new.

— Bhagavad Gita

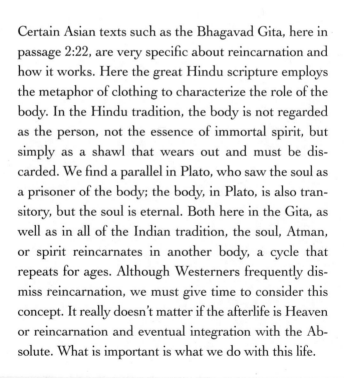

Certain Asian texts such as the Bhagavad Gita, here in passage 2:22, are very specific about reincarnation and how it works. Here the great Hindu scripture employs the metaphor of clothing to characterize the role of the body. In the Hindu tradition, the body is not regarded as the person, not the essence of immortal spirit, but simply as a shawl that wears out and must be discarded. We find a parallel in Plato, who saw the soul as a prisoner of the body; the body, in Plato, is also transitory, but the soul is eternal. Both here in the Gita, as well as in all of the Indian tradition, the soul, Atman, or spirit reincarnates in another body, a cycle that repeats for ages. Although Westerners frequently dismiss reincarnation, we must give time to consider this concept. It really doesn't matter if the afterlife is Heaven or reincarnation and eventual integration with the Absolute. What is important is what we do with this life.

[311]

Cease doing evil. Learn to do good,
search for justice, discipline the violent,
be just to the orphan, plead for the widow.

— Isaiah

⌒

Isaiah (1:16–17), the prophet of Israel, sums up in this powerful passage the moral heart of Judaism, Christianity, and Islam. It is instruction on the task of cultivating a good heart, one that is open and responsive to the poor, the orphans, and the widows. It emphasizes the path of justice, which naturally requires a rejection of evil. More important, it demands that each of us control our own inner violence, that discipline begin in our thoughts. The prophets of Israel focused on two points: faithfulness to God and his covenant with the people, and justice, which involves conversion of the heart. The latter teaching is the substance of social justice in the three faiths of the Book: Christianity, Judaism, and Islam. And a similar teaching on the necessity of an inner emphasis on justice is found in most religions.

Life is always a moral question that lies before us
sweetly, dependent on our gratitude and constant
struggle to cause as little suffering as possible
to all and everything around us.

— Paul Hawken

⌣

The harm we do the world around us doesn't often enter into our business considerations in America. But Paul Hawken, an entrepreneur, environmentalist, and author of the groundbreaking book *The Ecology of Commerce: A Declaration of Sustainability,* puts this question at the center of all our dealings, just as Jainism and Buddhism have done. The question is how to minimize as much as possible the suffering we cause. This is a question and a spiritual practice with which we are always dealing. It is never absent from our lives if we live consciously and authentically. The practice of nonharming stems from the spiritual realization of interdependence, the gratitude we feel to the earth and one another. It challenges us to discipline our thoughts and actions to minimize the harm we do to nature, other species, and the human community. Although we can never completely erase the harm we inflict in this imperfect existence, we can minimize it through thoughtful practice.

[313]

*The destiny of humanity . . . is a process of going back
to the source and origin. And that source and origin
is a supreme state of independence, [a] supreme state
of consciousness, transcending all vexing limitations,
infinite, boundless, eternal, beyond time and space.*

— Swami Chidananda

His Holiness Sri Swami Chidananda of the Hindu tradition is the leading spiritual teacher of the Divine Life
Society in the lineage of the great Swami Sivananda of
Rishikesh in North India. Here he leads us to a central
metaphysical and mystical realization of the Vedantic
tradition, the depth understanding of Indian esotericism. The Vedanta is a wisdom stream extending from
the *rishis,* the sages of ancient India, whose experiential,
contemplative understanding is communicated in the
four Vedas and the Upanishads. All mysticism is about
connecting with the origin, the original, timeless condition, the "supreme state of independence" (from this
conditioned, impermanent life and world) and the
"supreme state of consciousness" that is ultimate and
unchanging. This state is free of such limitations as corruption, change, ignorance, death, illness, and old age.
All of us come from this eternal, infinite, boundless
Reality that transcends space and time.

You can't say to a person, "Your cynicism is destructive."
You have to show them the way of delight,
the way of joy, the way of poetry —
and let the chips fall where they may.

— Robert Aitken Roshi

We can preach about enlightenment all we want, but people only take on the spiritual journey when they glimpse the joy it can hold. Robert Aitken Roshi is a Zen master based in Hawaii. His wisdom arises out of an illuminated state of awareness originating in his Zen meditation practice. From the depth of his inner experience, Aitken Roshi knows the cause for joy in being, the source of poetry, and "the way of true delight" in what is. This is what Zen reveals to the committed practitioner. Cynicism, as a life posture, is not an argument, but an excuse not to trust and hope, an unwillingness to be surprised by inspiration and joy. When we know someone trapped in cynicism, we can't persuade them out of it through logic; we must expose them to the delight, joy, and genuine poetry that we experience when we're in touch with the real.

If ever I get the chance to sit down with
The-One-Who-Owns-My-Heart, from
fortune's cup I'll drink my wine and
from the Garden of Union gather flowers.

— Hafiz

Like his fellow Sufi mystical poet Rumi, Hafiz challenges us to think and be in terms of the Divine Lover. He expresses his great jubilation at his total commitment to Allah, "The-One-Who-Owns-My-Heart." Hafiz is intoxicated with the Divine; he cannot help himself because he has been invaded by the Divine Lover. He knows no other way to happiness. He realizes that only Allah is, so he can no longer look to any other source to nourish his life, his hope, his aspirations for happiness. He has known the bliss of union, and once it is tasted one can no longer be satisfied by the joys of this passing world, the place of impermanence. Gathering flowers is a contemplative act associated with joy, optimism, and the hope of ultimate beatitude. Hafiz has espied those realities and communicates them to us in his exalted utterance. Do you wish to drink from the streams of Divine Union?

Our innate gifts are given. They come from a journey
that has spanned billions of years of life.

— Maya Tiwari

⌒

Our talents, according to Maya Tiwari, author of *A Life of Balance,* are part of the unfolding of this universe, the evolution of galaxies, stars, planets, the earth, and all life. These gifts are innate capacities granted to us in this gradual development of the cosmic community, but they have their ultimate origin in the Source itself, the mysterious principle from which all things spring. Whatever the Source is, however it is named or imagined, the truth is the same: Our gifts are donated from that originating point. Each interpretive system of spiritual and mystical culture understands this. The crucial point in life is to use these gifts wisely: not to squander them, but to commit them to the benefit of the whole community of life.

[317]

But those who know the Real is,
and know the unreal is not,
they shall indeed reach the Truth,
safe on the path of right thought.

— Dhammapada

All who know the Real from their own inner, or mystical, contemplative experience and practice, as the Dhammapada tells us in verse 1:12, have an absolute certitude about the Real or the Ultimate. They understand from the authenticity of their own experiential breakthroughs that "the unreal is not" and can never be, since the Real is. They are secure on the road of *right thought,* or *right view (samma ditthi),* as it is called in Buddhism's Noble Eightfold Path. To reach *right view,* one must come to the understanding of the nature of reality that springs from right mindfulness or spiritual practice. An inner peace, joy, and calmness of being are essential attributes of such a person's life, animating all of his or her activities.

To be looking elsewhere for miracles is to me
a sure sign of ignorance that everything is miraculous.

— Abraham Maslow

Abraham Maslow, a great psychologist of human potential, here echoes Albert Einstein, who said, "There are only two ways to live your life. One is as though nothing is a miracle. The other is as though everything is a miracle." The recognition that "everything is miraculous" is the knowledge of the mystic. It takes considerable awareness to bring home this point to ourselves, and yet everything declares it to us if we could only realize it. Maslow's wisdom tells us that if people are searching for the miraculous outside of themselves, they are in a state of ignorance. To be more conscious of the miraculous, we need to cultivate our awareness in each moment.

As one works, one finds what Carl Jung called
incredible synchronicities, which is really a term
for little miracles. And sometimes they're big miracles.

— Michael Harner

We all experience synchronicities in our lives, but usually if we notice them at all, we don't regard them as miracles. Michael Harner, author of *The Way of the Shaman,* puts them in the context of the miraculous. The power of our social conditioning in this culture clearly separates the sacred from the secular and the everyday. When we are working in and committed to the stream of goodness, we inevitably encounter miracles in the form of unexplainable synchronicities. There are other orders of reality and being at work in this world. The key is to recognize them and show gratitude for them.

No matter where you are, remember that forgiveness offers you peace of mind and everything else you could possibly ever want or hope for. It is an elixir, giving you your wholeness and leading you into the heart of God....

— Gerald Jampolsky

Gerald Jampolsky is a psychiatrist, founder of the Center for Attitudinal Healing, and author of *Forgiveness: The Greatest Healer of All.* Here he inspires us with his wise understanding of how central forgiveness is to our psychological and spiritual well-being. We all know we must forgive and never cease forgiving whenever it is necessary, yet it often feels like we're giving in or losing something. Yet if we do not forgive, then we are held back in our psychological, emotional, moral, and spiritual development. We must begin by forgiving ourselves and move on from there. As Dr. Jampolsky remarks, forgiveness brings us into wholeness and into greater relationship with God. May we all develop the ability to forgive ourselves and others.

Every day we are engaged in a miracle
which we don't even recognize: a blue sky, white clouds,
green leaves, the black, curious eyes of a child
— our own two eyes. All is a miracle.

— Thich Nhat Hanh

It is the poet's genius to recognize the miraculous in the beautiful physical details of everyday life. This saintly Vietnamese monk, a real interspiritual Buddhist who is also a poet, calls our attention to the miraculous by pointing it out in everyday beauties we can all understand. Children know this innately and unself-consciously. For most of us, life has become so ordinary, and routine has blinded us to the mysterious and the miracle that each day represents. When I go for a walk on the bike path along Lake Michigan in Chicago, I am often overwhelmed and inspired by the miracles I see: the seagulls flying or congregating on the beach in their communities; the nearby cautious crows; the drifting, ethereal quality of clouds; the vegetation that shifts shapes as the wind blows through; and the endless stream of fellow people on the bike path who walk, run, and cycle by. All are miraculous, but I only see the miracles when I look through the eyes of contemplation.

Friend, hope for the Guest while you are alive,
jump into experience while you are alive!
Think ... and think ... while you are alive.
What you call "salvation"
belongs to the time before death....
If you make love with the divine now, in the next life
you will have the face of satisfied desire.

— Kabir

A celebrated mystic poet of India, claimed by both Hindus and Muslims, Kabir remained aloof from both
communities. Here he presents us with an urgent view
of the mystic life. We have to know God now, not simply after death. Now is the time, in this life, to seek the
mystical path that leads into intimacy and union with
the Divine One. If we prepare ourselves, the Guest will
visit us. We have an opportunity to experience this
extraordinary reality while we are alive; we must not
wait until we pass from these shores. The mystic way
requires activation in this life, according to Kabir, and
bears fruit in true fulfillment.

Spirituality is not what we think about God or theology,
it's participation. That's all it is.

— Anne Wilson Schaef

⌒

Although spirituality depends on reflection, Anne
Wilson Schaef, author of *Beyond Therapy, Beyond Science,*
identifies an equally important aspect: participation or
interaction with one another within the greater mystery of existence. Participation demands hard work in
the process of our transformation. While spirituality
requires practice, primarily a solitary activity, the fullness of the spiritual life involves relationships with others and participation in their struggles, vulnerabilities,
and joys. This is *living* spirituality.

[324]

We have to go beyond the rational mind and the ego.
As long as you are in your rational mind,
you are still in the sphere of the ego,
and that limits you; eventually, it imprisons you.

— Bede Griffiths

⌒

Bede Griffiths, who spent nearly forty years in India
becoming free of his ego, understood the trap of the
rational mind. While he valued the place of reason in
his life and education, his attempts to grapple with the
world, experience, and the mystery of existence took
him beyond a simple reliance on it to find greater
understanding in his intuitive capacity. We get impris-
oned in our rational minds and the jail of the ego. The
ego keeps us from real growth. It blinds us to others.
and to the larger reality beyond ourselves. By disciplin-
ing the ego and augmenting the rational faculty, we can
develop the whole person.

[325]

Love and mercy apply to everybody,
no matter how much we want to hate them.

— Bo Lozoff

Bo Lozoff, author of *We're All Doing Time: A Time for Getting Free,* understands the basic responsibility we all have to practice compassion, particularly in the most difficult instances. In his work with his Human Kindness Foundation, an organization that brings spiritual practice to prisoners, he has seen the devastating results of lives based on hate. In every situation, compassion is appropriate. We have this responsibility even to people who hurt us. If we are going to grow into the fullness of our potential in our spiritual lives, we have to take this path of love, kindness, mercy, compassion, and true empathy. These qualities define us as individuals who have awakened within and care without. We often meet people who irritate us, or stir our negative emotions, but they are entitled to receive our compassion, and we are bound to the law of love and mercy. We cannot hold back.

The shape things take is not within your power;
the motives of your actions are.

— Sri Nisargadatta Maharaj

Sri Nisargadatta Maharaj, an Indian spiritual master, gives us some very practical wisdom on the subtleties of detachment to guide us through our lives. It is very true that we cannot determine events alone or control the actions of others. We cannot make peace between Israelis and Palestinians. We just don't have that kind of power. But the motives that guide our own actions are definitely within our sphere of control. No matter what is going on around us, we can still have meaningful reasons for our behavior — reasons that reflect our integrity, passion, and joy. We can decide to take a course, in all our actions, that demonstrates a moral and spiritual maturity. End results are beyond our control, but our inner life is not.

To love is to think, speak, and act
according to the spiritual knowledge
that we are infinitely loved by God
and called to make that love visible in the world.

— Henri Nouwen

Again we explore the notion of reciprocal love with the Divine with this quotation from Henri Nouwen, a Dutch priest, psychologist, and spiritual writer. That the Divine's love for us is the basis of our love in practice is an essential insight of the Christian tradition. The utter primacy of love is the guiding absolute of Christian motivation, attitudes, thoughts, speech, and actions. It is this ultimate love that inspires, energizes, and shapes the cosmos, nature, and the human family. To experience the Divine in its deepest sense is to experience the love it has for us. And to know this love gives us the capacity to love God in return, as well as to love others. Again, it is the Source. As we imbibe Divine Love, as we evolve in its depth and transforming urgency, it increases our ability to love in all aspects of our lives.

[328]

Properly speaking, awake is not really awake because the golden eternity never went to sleep: you can tell by the constant sound of Silence which cuts through this world like a magic diamond through the trick of your not realizing that your mind caused the world.

— Jack Kerouac

The great Beat icon Jack Kerouac put a wild and wonderfully American spin on Buddhist philosophy that inspired an entire generation to explore Asia's religious traditions. In his inimitable Beat poetic style, he here suggests that the awakened state is always awake, and it is our innate, natural condition if we would get beyond our own sleep. The "golden eternity" is always awake; it's we who are asleep. He focuses on the perpetual sound of silence to reveal the awakened state, the ultimate nature of the mind that never sleeps. This mind creates our world, or as Kerouac says, "…your mind caused the world."

If we trust our intuition and respond, it's always right,
because we're open enough to see what to do.

— Paul Horn

As celebrated musician Paul Horn describes here, opening to intuition isn't just a matter of trusting voices in our head; it's a state of alert openness that results in better decisions. He encourages us to trust intuition and not to resist or dismiss it. Results will turn out well because we are following a way of knowledge, rather than a whim. Being open to what is, we will know what to do, as we permit ourselves to be led by our intuition. It takes some of us many years to gather sufficient wisdom to really trust our intuition and learn to respond to it positively. Many great breakthroughs, discoveries, visionary theories, and works of art, music, and philosophy are the fruit of trusting intuition and responding to the course it reveals.

[330]

*Everything in the universe is energy or a manifestation
of energy, and the purpose of spiritual work is to
become one with that flow of higher creative energy
coming from God through the cosmos.*

— Rudi

Swami Rudrananda, or Rudi (born Albert Rudolph), is
a Hindu spiritual teacher who used to teach a circle of
disciples in New York City and has influenced countless
souls. His statement is curiously modern, even reflecting
a scientific spirit, and clearly influencing many New Age
adherents. But the teaching is also a classic insight of the
Hindu mystical and ascetic tradition, which parallels
the understanding of the Taoist sages. Material forms,
especially organic ones, are mutable — they are born,
develop, and decay away; but energy is permanent. As
physics tells us, energy can be neither created nor
destroyed. Energy is always changing its form, but as
energy itself, it remains the same. We also know that
matter is really frozen light or concentrated energy. The
Divine is this energy, this light that is the ground of
everything that is. Becoming attuned to this Divine
Energy, uniting with it, and allowing it to transform us
into it, is the goal for each of us.

A person has no religion who has not
slowly and painfully gathered one together,
adding to it, shaping it.

— D. H. Lawrence

⌒

The great British writer D. H. Lawrence, speaking from his own experience, gives us some very practical wisdom about *authentic* religion. It is essential to be active and creative in assimilating a faith tradition. Spirituality, or authentic religion, dawns when the individual takes control of his or her spiritual life. If religion is a passive affair in which the person simply goes to church, synagogue, temple, or mosque out of mechanical commitment, then it has little meaning beyond community. Religion and spirituality by definition have to engage the whole person, especially the inner life. We have to take a religion to ourselves, shape and add to it from our own experience, learning, and aspirations. Then it becomes something of great value.

[332]

*A vital faith is more like an organism
or a work of art than it is like a cafeteria tray.*
— Huston Smith

Although he is a great proponent of synthesis in the study of religion, Huston Smith, the venerable sage of the religious and spiritual life as well as comparative religion, corroborates D. H. Lawrence's insight but adds that authentic spirituality cannot simply be a grab bag of beliefs and practices. A faith that really means something in a person's life, a faith that nourishes and inspires, that is a source of insight, strength, encouragement, and guidance, needs to be cultivated, protected, never taken for granted. Such a faith doesn't happen without sufficient effort and commitment. In this sense, it is similar to a living being. Insofar as we cultivate our faith and permit it to be the center of our lives and the animating core of our being and value, it becomes, as Smith says, "a work of art."

[333]

*If you do spiritual practice without performing selfless
actions, it will be like building a house without any doors.*

— Mata Amritanandamayi

Mata Amritanandamayi, the hugging guru, zeros in on
the essential truth of engaged spirituality. We cannot
simply be concerned with our spiritual development
without any connection to compassionate service or
selfless action. Prayer, meditation, indeed any spiritual
practice is certainly essential, but it must be augmented
by engaging the heart. Compassionate deeds, kindness,
mercy, and reaching out to others are required of all of
us who desire to be on the path of wisdom.

[334]

People imagine that they communicate their virtue or
vice only by overt actions, and do not see that virtue
or vice emit a breath at every moment.

— Ralph Waldo Emerson

⌒

You simply can't fake it! The transcendent American
transcendentalist Ralph Waldo Emerson here outlines
one of the subtleties of moral character. Virtue and vice
emanate an effect that can be detected. The virtuous
express their goodness of character in who they are,
and not simply in what they do. Virtue and vice are
both habits that in a sense, cultivated over time, emit a
feeling. Virtue is also the path that leads to happiness,
which as Aristotle says, "accompanies virtuous activity." In other words, we are only really happy in the
long run if we are committed to virtue, allowing our
character to be schooled and formed by its precious
wisdom. When we are truly in harmony with the
Divine, others, nature, and ourselves, we are naturally
virtuous and others will know it!

[335]

Be a blazing fire of truth,
be a beauteous blossom of love,
and be a soothing balm of peace.

— Sufi saying

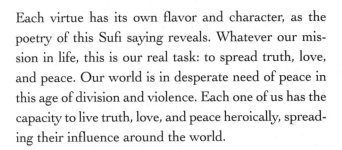

Each virtue has its own flavor and character, as the poetry of this Sufi saying reveals. Whatever our mission in life, this is our real task: to spread truth, love, and peace. Our world is in desperate need of peace in this age of division and violence. Each one of us has the capacity to live truth, love, and peace heroically, spreading their influence around the world.

To those who believe and do deeds of righteousness
hath Allah promised forgiveness and a great reward.

— The Qur'an

Misinterpretation of this passage from the Holy
Qur'an (sura 10:19) has led to considerable violence
and heartache, yet in reality it expresses the basic
moral awareness of the Islamic tradition. Having faith
or trust in Allah, the Divine, seeking to be always compassionate and loving in action toward others, and pursuing holiness, a total conformity to the Divine Will,
represent the heart of Islam's understanding of religious and spiritual life. By holding to this ideal, one
merits Allah's mercy, forgiveness, and reward of Paradise, to be with God forever. The true Muslim is one
who strives to emulate Allah's capacity for mercy and
compassion, faithfulness, kindness, and availability.

There is a bridge between time and Eternity; and this bridge is Atman, the Spirit in us.... To one who goes over that bridge, the night becomes like day, because in the worlds of the Spirit there is a Light which is everlasting.

— Chandogya Upanishad

This passage from Chandogya Upanishad 8.4.1 concentrates on the pivotal reality and nature of the eternal Atman, the immanent presence of the Divine One, the Brahman, in all things. It is the inner principle of life, being, and consciousness in all sentient entities. It is the very continuity between this existence and the everlasting reality of the Source. The person who awakens to the Atman, crossing the bridge between time and eternity, discovers the Divine Light, the everlasting truth of the Brahman, the light in which there is no darkness.

Lord Buddha's admonition to us was (to serve)
by helping those who suffer physically to overcome
physical suffering, those who are in fear to overcome fear,
those who suffer mentally to overcome mental suffering.
Be of service to all living beings.

— A. T. Ariyaratne

A. T. Ariyaratne — venerable Buddhist layman, social and spiritual activist, founder of the Sarvodaya movement in Sri Lanka — succinctly expresses the Buddha's teaching on practical compassion: removing the suffering of sentient beings. Although some non-Buddhists misidentify Buddhist practice as solely concentrating on personal enlightenment at the expense of service to others, this pioneer of socially engaged Buddhism identifies the true heart of Buddhist philosophy. Dr. Ariyaratne followed in the footsteps of Gandhi and King by creating a nonviolent movement of reform of the social, political, and economic conditions of his people. The name of his movement, Sarvodaya, is a Sanskrit term used by Gandhi that means *awakening all*. Following this Buddhist path, Ariyaratne has attempted to remove the economic, social, and political sources of his people's suffering.

[339]

Remove the sandals from your feet,
for the place where you stand is holy ground.

— Exodus

⁓

This celebrated passage of the Book of Exodus (3:5)
chronicles Moses's first encounter with Yahweh, when
Moses experienced the Divine in the burning bush. It
can be extended, however, to all instances in which we
encounter the Sacred, no matter what religion we follow. At Mount Sinai, where the manifestation of God
appeared in the form of a burning bush that was not
consumed, a standard for holy ground was established.
In our own lives, holy ground may include an altar in
our bedroom, a closet that has become a sanctuary, a
special place in our backyard, a park bench in the city.
These places are made holy by our spiritual experience,
but we must, in a sense, remove our shoes — to show
our respect, but more importantly to help make ourselves a conduit for the sacred. The Divine Presence is
everywhere; it only requires us to experience it.

Beloved, let us love one another, because love is of God;
everyone who loves is begotten by God and knows God.
Whoever is without love does not know God,
for God is love.

— First Letter of John

It cannot be said too often that God is love. In the First Letter of John (4:7–8), this key to the mystery and truth of the Christian faith is stated with simple, direct eloquence. To follow this absolute path with consistency is difficult, for many forces in the world work against such a commitment. But if we love selflessly and get out of the way, we are said to be sons and daughters of God, or as John says, "begotten by God." If we truly love one another in this way then we "know God." John makes it clear that without love, a person simply "does not know God." To say that "God is love" is to express a mystical truth about the nature of the Divinity. The inner reality, core focus, commitment, and intention of God is love itself.

The community is created, not when people come
together in the name of religion, but when they come
together bringing honesty, respect, and kindness
to support an awakening of the sacred.

— Jack Kornfield

As a founding teacher of the wonderful Spirit Rock Meditation Center, Buddhist teacher and author Jack Kornfield knows the demands of community. While common orientation and commitment to a particular religion can be helpful, something more is required: the mature qualities of honesty, mutual respect, and kindness. They are what make community happen; they become the glue of daily life. They also allow a space to emerge where members can awaken to or realize the presence of the sacred. A community can have a solid commitment to a religious tradition, a teacher, and a spiritual practice, but much of what we are seeking in the spiritual process is basic honesty, mutual respect, kindness, compassion, and sensitivity to one another. Tension and disagreement naturally arise in any community. To overcome them requires uncommon courage and flexibility, hallmarks of those following a true spiritual path.

Be melting snow; wash yourself of yourself.

— Rumi

⌒

A famous Zen teaching tells the practitioner: If you meet
the Buddha in the road, kill him. Although this koan-like
teaching can have many interpretations, or no rational
interpretation at all, to me it speaks of what the great
Tibetan Buddhist teacher Chögyam Trungpa called
"spiritual materialism," where the ego latches on to spiritual practice as another method of aggrandizement.
Rumi, the great master of the inner journey, lyrically
captures the necessity of selflessness, the abandonment
of self and self-preoccupation. "To wash yourself of
yourself" refers to the Sufi teaching on *fana,* annihilation
of the self, losing oneself in God, becoming as nothing in
order to awaken into the fullness of life in the Divine, or
what the Sufi tradition calls *baqa,* unification in and with
God, or Allah. If we are like melting snow, we will be
free of ourselves because we will *let go* of ourselves. Ironically, if we are not careful, spirituality can actually bol-
ster our ego, rather than annihilate it. Be vigilant!

[343]

There is no light without shadow and no psychic
wholeness without imperfection. To round itself
out, life calls not for perfection but for completeness.

— Carl Jung

⁓

Nature writer Barry Lopez, in an acknowledgment of
life's inherent darkness, called the task of this existence
"making your life a worthy expression of a leaning into
the light." Carl Jung, the celebrated pioneer of the unconscious psyche, identifies the shadow of the healthy
self as an essential part of wholeness of identity. Perfection is an ideal toward which we strive, but it is actually
a property belonging to the Divine. Philosophically, we
have to remember that wholeness can only be known
and pursued in relation to its opposite, imperfection,
the shadow side of our nature. How can we experience
joy and happiness unless we know sorrow? How can
we identify growth and beauty unless we also know
decay? And how can we achieve genuine love and
goodness unless we see what it must struggle against?

[344]

What are you going to do with your personality,
bury it?
You can't bury it; it's like nuclear waste.

— Ram Dass

We can work with our personality, but we cannot jetti-
son or repress our demons; we cannot flee from their
truths. Spiritual teacher Ram Dass echoes the previous
passage from Carl Jung by emphasizing how much the
negative aspects of our personality are part of us. When
one tries to deny his personality's imperfections, they
only come back stronger. We really need to accept, con-
secrate, and integrate with the higher dimensions of the
self. We should celebrate our personalities, even their
shadow elements. The more we embrace ourselves, the
more whole we become.

[345]

When one person heals, the rest of the world
is deeply affected. We don't heal alone.

— Diane Cirincione

We are all connected to one another in an essential, intrinsic interdependence. What happens to any one of us has a direct effect on the totality of relationships in the body of humanity. Co-author of *Love Is the Answer: Creating Positive Relationships,* Diane Cirincione articulates this truth, found in the teachings of all the great world religions. The interconnectedness of all sentient beings within the cosmos is what I like to call the Divine Matrix. Our healing, in some intangible but very real way, brings healing to the world, though we may not perceive it. Our healing, in this sense, is a corporate event and process that involves all. This is one reason why prayer is so important to the healing process: It engages others, perhaps even the totality, in our healing. The benefits that emerge, though invisible, are nonetheless real.

The past is not dead; it is not even past.

— William Faulkner

~

Consider the Middle East, which is so dominated by the past, or the conflict in Northern Ireland, which is still unresolved after centuries of discord. Examine the tensions between Hindu and Muslim communities in India or Christian and Muslim communities in the Sudan. The past, particularly the religious past and its fears, is still very much present. It is very hard to overcome history and to reconcile the past so that it doesn't impinge on the present and the future. It takes enormous effort, patience, and inspired dialogue. It requires a willingness to heal, rather than forget. To heal is to become free of the hold of the past. Healing the past, and thus putting it finally aside, requires generosity from the two conflicting communities or individuals involved. It requires a generous spirit that seeks reconciliation and a building of mutual respect and trust.

*The new spirituality is a spirituality of illuminating
our daily lives with what we call the divine,
and recognizing that in ourselves.*

— Riane Eisler

The great proponent of the partnership model, which
rejects the necessity of domination, Riane Eisler looks
in the direction of the ordinary to define and understand what spirituality is all about. What she calls "the
new spirituality" involves a transfiguration of ordinary,
everyday life, of the experiences we all have in common. This new spirituality is not about religion but
about illuminating the ordinary aspects of daily life to
reveal the Divine. It is about the simplicity of tending
a garden, of watching birds, of playing with our children, of looking into one another's eyes, or of washing
dishes, cooking, walking, or reading. It is also about
taking in the vast mystery of the universe, about our
dreams and inner stirrings, our experiences with meditation and prayer. In these experiences, the Divine is
manifesting itself, communicating itself to us, and trans-
mitting to us its wisdom and grace.

There is no such thing as evil, only ignorance.

— Irina Tweedie

⌒

Calling our enemies evil is always easier than looking at the root cause of their actions. Irina Tweedie, author of *Daughter of Fire,* presents us with the Eastern understanding of evil and sin. The philosophies of the East reject the notion of ontological evil — that there is a source of evil, or that persons actually embrace evil for themselves or willingly become instruments of this ugly reality, no matter the form it takes. Properly speaking, no person, no matter how depraved, chooses evil for its own sake. When a person decides on an evil action or course, it is because they see some good in it for themselves. The problem is that their choice is saturated by their own ignorance: of the nature of the good itself, of the necessity not to harm others, and of how their actions ultimately harm not only their enemies but themselves. Evil so conceived is always a matter of ignorance.

[349]

*What does the Lord require of you but to do justice
and to love kindness, and to walk humbly with your God?*

— Micah

I have always loved this biblical teaching because it is
so accessible to all of us. This powerful, eloquently succinct teaching from the Prophet Micah (6:8) in a very
simple and direct way sums up for us what God
expects of us in our deepest commitments of virtue,
attitude, and action. To be just, kind, and humble
before the Divine is a possibility for everyone, even
atheists, if they're willing to live with ambiguity and an
open mind about the Ultimate Mystery. No matter
what we believe, we are all bound to seek justice, to
think and act with genuine kindness, and to have
humility of heart. To seek to be just in all situations, to
do justice in society and to pursue it for the sake of the
vulnerable, is our first edict. The law of treating all sentient beings with kindness should govern our interactions with all others in life. To walk with humility in the
sight of God is the ultimate commitment.

*Ultimately, what we are looking to is the deepest
connection within ourselves. As we get more
connected to that, we begin to feel in harmony
with other people and with the rest of the world.*

— Shakti Gawain

Author of *Creative Visualization,* Shakti Gawain focuses
in the above statement on an essential principle of
growth and the process of emerging into real maturity.
We have to know ourselves deeply and comprehensively. When we identify "the deepest connection
within ourselves" we will notice immediately that it is
what ties us to everyone and everything else. We discover we are not actually separate from anyone or anything; we are intimately connected with all. This is a
profoundly liberating realization — an overpowering,
overarching principle in every tradition. Finding our
inner connection with ourselves then reveals our connection with everyone else. It's that simple, although
this discovery and realization takes great effort and perseverance. Once found, it cannot be taken for granted.

Wherever space pervades, my wisdom mind is present.
My compassion now outshines the sun.
Greater are my blessings than the following clouds,
and swifter than the rain I bring accomplishments.

— Yeshe Tsogyal

Many regard Yeshe Tsogyal (757–817) as the mother of the Tibetan Buddhist tradition. Little is known in the West of this extraordinary being, whose name means *ocean of primordial wisdom,* but she is a towering figure in Tibet. In this lyrical passage, she compares her enlightened capacities to the most admired natural forces. Her consciousness is as vast as the universe and beyond, and her capacity for compassion is more radiant than the sun. She is completely realized in her Buddha-nature, in touch with the unconditioned, eternal nature of the mind, the caring ability of the inner reality of awareness. We are all blessed with this vast mine of infinite compassion if we open ourselves to our true nature. Then our blessings and accomplishments become as swift and effective as Yeshe Tsogyal's.

For of the soul the body form doth take:
For soul is form, and doth the body make.

— Edmund Spenser

In his Shakespearian tongue, Edmund Spenser (1552–99), the great English poet, speaks a truth known since Aristotle and Thomas Aquinas. The soul is the form of the body; it is the guiding principle of its development, and more basically still, it is what vivifies the body. The body's form follows the soul's nature, and the body only exists because of the *ensouling* reality of spirit. The poet shows how we must strive to live in the soul within our bodies, to be open to its wisdom and its ability to form a bridge between time and eternity. Bede Griffiths often remarked, "The point of life is for the body to submit to the soul, and the soul to submit to the spirit." This approach is the anthropology of the New Testament, how it understands the nature of the human. In a sense, life is a process of becoming attuned to your soul. Do not neglect this essential work!

We must not wish anything other than what happens
from moment to moment, all the while,
however, exercising ourselves in goodness.

— St. Catherine of Genoa

Again we find a statement we might first identify as Buddhist coming from the mouth of a great Christian saint. St. Catherine of Genoa (1447–1510), born Caterinetta Fieschi, brings us back to the utter importance of the now, the present moment, each moment. In each moment the will of God is present, if we can only allow ourselves to discern it. Part of that will is that we accept wholly what is presented to us, without resistance. If we encounter a homeless person, an annoying stranger, a difficult relative, or a combative associate at work, our task is to be present to them and to respond with compassion, or as Catherine says so well, to "exercise ourselves in goodness." There is in this wonderful teaching a kind of "Taoist Catholicism" at work. As we discern the Divine Will in each moment, we must align ourselves with it. Being kind, loving, compassionately available, and responsive are ways to exercise this goodness.

On the raft of good company alone
you will cross over the vast ocean of samsara.

— Srimad Bhagavatam

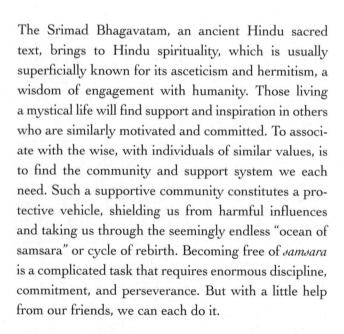

The Srimad Bhagavatam, an ancient Hindu sacred text, brings to Hindu spirituality, which is usually superficially known for its asceticism and hermitism, a wisdom of engagement with humanity. Those living a mystical life will find support and inspiration in others who are similarly motivated and committed. To associate with the wise, with individuals of similar values, is to find the community and support system we each need. Such a supportive community constitutes a protective vehicle, shielding us from harmful influences and taking us through the seemingly endless "ocean of samsara" or cycle of rebirth. Becoming free of *samsara* is a complicated task that requires enormous discipline, commitment, and perseverance. But with a little help from our friends, we can each do it.

[355]

Zen, in a word, is simply "Emptying."... One who is fully emptied in Zen finds oneself in everything, literally, and is able to identify fully with everything, to be all things, and thus to act in total freedom, according to what the particular situation demands. Such a one is no longer separated by the illusory barrier between himself and the "Other."

— Ruben Habito

Ruben Habito, a professor at Southern Methodist University and author of *Living Zen, Loving God,* is a Christian roshi (Zen Buddhist master), a genuine interspiritual teacher. Here Habito teaches the importance of a nondiscriminating mind and how cultivating that state of mind eventually leads to *samadhi* or enlightenment. Becoming empty of ego and an obsession with concepts allows us to experience the true nature of existence. When we are empty, our capacity for connection increases, and we act from an inner ground of freedom, rather than from selfish desires that arise from the ego. When our boundaries expand beyond this limited identity, we realize our connection with everything.

The oldest brother or sister is born first,
but the wise person anytime.

— African adage

⌒

This African aphorism is a proverb from the Bamileke tribe of West Cameroon, and it expresses that wisdom can dawn in an individual at any time. In most cultures, wisdom is naturally associated with elders because of their long experience, but old age doesn't necessarily translate into wisdom. Children sometimes convey a wisdom that comes *through* them rather than *from* them, and St. Benedict says in his Holy Rule that the community should always ask the view of the youngest in the community on any issue the monks or nuns are considering, because God often speaks through youth. Often, those who are more open to new ideas and intuitive wisdom, those without the buildup of years of assumptions, can prove best that wisdom is ageless.

[357]

You're bound to become a Buddha if you practice.
If water drips long enough even rocks wear through.

— Shih-wu

The Chinese Buddhist sage Shih-wu (1272–1352) reminds us of the wisdom of a persevering, disciplined practice. Just as dripping water wears away the hardest rock, spiritual practice refines us and wears away the obstacles to enlightenment. These obstacles include ignorance, craving, selfish desire, and confusion about reality. The primary obstacle, however, is one's own self, particularly our inordinate attachment to the ego and personality. Steady practice combined with proper motivation leads into our Buddha-nature. Experience through the millennia related to awakening and transformation has brought to the forefront of practical method and wisdom the primacy or effectiveness of spiritual practice, especially meditation. But as the Zen tradition emphasizes, enlightenment comes in its own time. It may take years of sitting before the lightning of a *kensho* experience arrives. It cannot be forced or coerced.

[358]

Hard times aren't the hurdles on the road to God,
they are the road.

— Martin Buber

Difficulties are opportunities in our journey to God. War, poverty, illness, the death of loved ones, work problems, petty misunderstandings, tensions in our relationships — all are golden opportunities for growth because they can open our hearts to reality. These difficulties challenge us, and we understandably try to avoid them, but they give us the material out of which we shape who we are in the deepest sense. They allow us to know our true selves rather than staying stuck in the superficial though tenacious ego. They dispose us to openness and surrender to the Divine; they soften and ripen us until we become receptive to grace and guidance of God.

Your trials did not come to punish you,
but to awaken you.

— Paramahansa Yogananda

⌒

The Eastern voice of the great Hindu sage Paramahansa Yogananda echoes the previous insight of
Western philosopher Martin Buber. Trials, difficulties, and challenges bring us to our senses about our
lives. They can serve as vehicles of realization, helping us to understand why we are here and how necessary the spiritual journey is for us. They awaken us to
the serious purpose of life and inspire us not to waste
this opportunity on a halfhearted existence. Yogananda understood from his own journey the place of
hardships, or trials, and he overcame them all, becoming a very effective spiritual teacher who has influenced the lives of thousands of followers around the
world. He knew what we all must come to know: Difficulties bring our attention to the deepest level of
awareness.

[360]

To know the sweetness of the Infinite within us,
that is the cause, the reason, the purpose,
the only purpose of our being.

— Nicholas of Cusa

⌒

Nicholas of Cusa, or Cusanus, presents here the ultimate perspective on our lives. Everything that happens here has an infinite significance. Each one of us has an infinite meaning and is part of the greater whole, the Infinite Reality, the Divine itself. We are here to know God, or as Cusanus says, "the sweetness of the Infinite within us," and this sweetness must saturate our understanding, our very beings. Our whole reason for being is to share in the sweetness of the Infinite, the inner life of the God-head. To realize the Divine Sweetness directly is the reason for our existence, since the Absolute Goodness wants to share its life with us. But again, to awaken to this realization requires a spiritual alertness that is shaped in living the inner life, taking the spiritual journey. Have you experienced this wonderful supernatural fragrance, this sweetness of the Infinite? Do you want to? Are you willing to change your life radically so you can? If you do, you will be happy always!

All we ever do our whole lives is go from
one little piece of Holy Ground to the next.

— J. D. Salinger

The pieces of holy ground that celebrated American writer J. D. Salinger refers to, the locations we discover on our earthly pilgrimage, can be traditional sacred places, centers of religious and spiritual power. They can also be mystical experiences that come in thousands of forms, each unique to the individual who experiences them. Sometimes they are thoughts, dreams, or philosophical illuminations. Other times they are inspirations, quiet moments in church, synagogue, mosque, or temple. Often they are moments of love between two people or moments when we observe great beauty. There are also times that the Holy comes through suffering, tragedy, and death. In whatever form the Holy reveals itself to us, we must be ready to receive its grace.

[362]

*The human body is His sitar. He draws the strings,
and out of it comes the music of the inner universe.*

— Kabir

Kabir was not simply an incomparable poet, but a deeply inspired sage. Weary of religions and religious institutions, this mystic spoke always from the authentic depths of his inner mysticism. Kabir compares us to a sitar, which the Divine One takes hold of to play its sacred music. He "draws" our strings that are in greater and greater harmony with his purpose. The Divine Universe authors this celestial music, which wasn't created by any human mind but has always existed and is part of us.

Living the spiritual life is the attitude you hold in your mind when you are down on your knees scrubbing the steps.

— Evelyn Underhill

Evelyn Underhill's monumental and influential work *Mysticism* was published in 1911. Although her wisdom was itself monumental, it can be captured in the simple, ordinary details of daily activity. She characterizes the spiritual life as a transfiguring attitude of humility that affects everything we do. Scrubbing floors, washing dishes, doing the laundry, raking leaves in the backyard, shopping for groceries — all are very simple activities, and all are occasions in which we can live with mindfulness and humility. Spirituality is an attitude, a disposition, something that permeates all aspects of our being and action, our relationships, and work — everything we do from the most simple to the most extraordinary.

[364]

Rituals channel your life energy toward the light.
Without the discipline of practice, you will tumble
constantly backward into darkness.

— Lao Tzu

The venerable Chinese sage Lao Tzu calls our attention back to the necessity of ritual — both formal religious ritual and the daily ritual of our personal practice, whether it be prayer, meditation, or something else. Such spiritual practice requires, or more accurately *is*, a discipline deeply situated in firm motivation. The more we are grounded in our spiritual practice, the more our energy is directed to the light, to the positive forces we work with in the course of our lives. It is in the regularity of our spiritual practice, our effort and our readiness, that we open ourselves both to the big, transformative breakthroughs and to steady, incremental progress along the path of illumination.

Eternity is the simultaneous possession of infinite life.

— Boethius

Boethius (480–525), a Roman philosopher, translator, and commentator on Aristotelian writings, gives us a succinct definition of eternity. Our experience of time is so fragmented. We encounter the moments of our life as successions, or frames of perception. It's somewhat analogous to the frames in a movie. We perceive our lives unfolding like a series of pictures before our eyes, day by day, moment by moment. In eternity there is no succession, no moment by moment, but only one integral moment, the Everlasting Now in which all moments are part of the absolute moment of the Now. All the moments of all lives in all worlds, in all realms and universes, are simultaneous with one another. It is like a great cosmic, heavenly banquet at which we are all present: everything that is, was, or could be. Let us all aspire to realize this Divine Consciousness, our birthright and our final home.

[ABOUT THE AUTHOR]

Brother Wayne Teasdale is a lay monk who combines the traditions of Christianity and Hinduism in the way of Christian Sannyasa. A leading activist and teacher in building common ground between religions, Teasdale serves on the board of trustees of the Parliament of the World's Religions and as a member of many other interfaith organizations. He is an adjunct professor at DePaul University, Columbia College, and the Catholic Theological Union and coordinator of the Bede Griffiths International Trust. He is the author of *The Mystic Heart: Discovering a Universal Spirituality in the World's Religions* and *A Monk in the World: Cultivating a Spiritual Life.* He holds an M.A. in philosophy from St. Joseph College and a Ph.D. in theology from Fordham University. He lives at the Catholic Theological Union in Chicago and speaks throughout the world.

New World Library is dedicated to
publishing books and audio products
that inspire and challenge us to improve
the quality of our lives and our world.

Our products are available
in bookstores everywhere.
For our catalog, please contact:

New World Library
14 Pamaron Way
Novato, California 94949

Phone: (415) 884-2100 or (800) 972-6657
Catalog requests: Ext. 50
Orders: Ext. 52
Fax: (415) 884-2199

E-mail: escort@newworldlibrary.com
Website: www.newworldlibrary.com